The Berkeley Rebellion And Beyond

The Berkeley Rebellion And Beyond

ESSAYS ON POLITICS AND EDUCATION IN THE TECHNOLOGICAL SOCIETY

by

SHELDON S. WOLIN

and

JOHN H. SCHAAR

A New York Review Book

DISTRIBUTED BY VINTAGE BOOKS
A DIVISION OF RANDOM HOUSE, INC

A NEW YORK REVIEW BOOK
Distributed by Vintage Books,
A Division of Random House, Inc.

Published by The New York Review
250 West 57th Street
New York, New York 10019

Library of Congress Catalog Card Number:
75-136480

All of the essays in this book originally
appeared in *The New York Review of Books.*

First printing August 1970
Printed in the U.S.A.

Contents

Introduction

The essays collected in this volume were written for *The New York Review* over the course of the last six years. During those years, American society moved into a time of troubles deeper than any since the Civil War, and American higher education plunged into storms more turbulent than any in its history. There are few signs that the storm is lifting: in so far as the campuses are barometers reflecting conditions outside, there is every sign of harder weather ahead.

Three of the essays center around events on the Berkeley campus of the University of California, where, it is generally agreed, the campus troubles began. Both authors were members of the Berkeley faculty for more than a decade, and reported events from that embattled position. Two of the essays survey scenes and events of broader scope. But even the "Reports from Berkeley" rested on the assumption that what was happening there was diagnostic of what was happening or might happen elsewhere. Hence, even the Berkeley essays discuss matters of more general scope. It became clear during these years that the Berkeley troubles had a broader meaning, but the question was, was Berkeley symptomatic or causal of maladies elsewhere? In either case, what began at Berkeley soon became epidemic. From Berkeley's Free Speech

Movement of 1964 to Kent State's massacre of 1970, over 300 campuses experienced degrees of disorder ranging in form from polite protest to savage violence, and ranging in content from questions of fairness in campus disciplinary hearings to university involvement in war, racism, and urban deterioration.

In attempting to make sense out of the events of these years we had to develop a theory–if that is not too pretentious a term for an improvised and sketchy set of metaphors, analogies, and concepts that seemed to bring order out of the confusion.

First of all, despite the great number and variety of institutions of higher education in this country, there are certain features of the Berkeley setting which give it a wider, more theoretical significance. Berkeley is a huge and inchoate educational organization governed not by custom and common experience but held together by rules and powered by money, as Clark Kerr, its chief architect, once said. It has 27,000 students and well over a thousand faculty, dozens of specialized research units, a heavy administrative structure, and an educational outlook attuned to the tempo and pressures of a dynamic state whose economy rests upon military and space operations, advanced agri-business, and the production of the means of recreation and entertainment. At the same time, the culture surrounding the campus offers the sharpest contrast to the organized society and its technological marvels: a culture that is youthful, disheveled, searching and experimental, and resolutely anti-vocational.

In its corporate and bureaucratic forms and in its dedication to the values of instrumental knowledge and technological growth, Berkeley education follows the pattern of contemporary American society, with its vast and interlocking corporate structures, its bureaucratic modes of handling human material, its replacement of substance by technique, and its commitment to efficiency, growth, and power. These parallels between university and society converge at critical points. Technological society is peculiarly the product of technical knowledge. It has no need (save ornamental) for modes of knowledge built on lived experience ordered by disciplined reflection and extended by moral and aesthetic sensibility. Universities have been deliberately organized and subsidized to manufacture technical knowledge. Further, technological society needs battalions of competent managers, skilled technicians, reliable clerks, and eager consumers, and it looks to the universities to supply them. In sum, the connections between the campus on the one side and economy, government, and society on the other have grown so close that the boundaries between them are hard to distinguish. This accelerating "economization" and "socialization" of the university during the last quarter-century proceeded with little protest or challenge. On the contrary: it was boosted in nearly all quarters as the key to progress and enlightenment.

As a result of these convergences and affiliations extraordinary happenings on the campus are likely to indicate or intimate troubles in the larger society, just as social and political rumbles are quickly transmitted to the campus. The Vietnam war is only the most spectacular example: student opposition to the draft foreshadowed public opposition to the war; recent cuts in the funds of the NIMH and the NSF, required by a war-strained budget, are seriously restricting research activities at many universities.

Nobody save a few purists and antiquarians worried much about the economization of the university. But when, beginning in 1964, the campuses showed signs of becoming politicized (meaning, of course, not the familiar exploitation of the university by government and semi-public bodies, but the growing awareness of and responsiveness to political issues by groups on campuses), then cries of pain and alarm were heard from all quarters. Politicization, it was claimed, would surely corrupt the university and reduce its social utility. What began as alarm had by 1970 grown into something very close to systematic policies of repression of political activity on campus.

Why this response? In part because Americans have little respect or affection for politics and those who practice it. In part because political action is regarded as the realm of passion, opinion, and prejudice–the very antitheses of the techno-bureaucratic culture, with its faith in objectivity and expertise. In part, too, because politics is perhaps the last preserve of public passions, now that religion is of small moment to anyone, including the new breed of seminarians.

But all these factors do not add up to an explanation either of the growing politicization of the campuses or of the increasingly heavy counter-assaults against that politicization. For a fuller explanation it is necessary to look once again at the close integration of campus and community.

The campuses are disturbed because American society itself is in profound crisis. There are special reasons–which we shall mention shortly–why the general crisis has taken the peculiar forms it has on campus, but the nature of the general crisis must first be identified.

It is a crisis both of values and of power. By a

paradoxical reversal-through-fulfillment, America's success in pursuing certain values by certain means has become America's failure. Having become the richest and most powerful nation in history, we can begin to see our poverty and weakness. After we have pursued the values of wealth and power to the near exclusion of all others, when they fail, how can any others help? The feeling grows, in Auden's words, that "All the values in the world won't save us / Although they give our crimes a certain air." And now we are no longer successful even at our crimes.

Ours is also a crisis of power in which the mightiest nation in the world, having passed some fatal limit, now watches its power grow ever less effectual in coping with the human environment and ever more destructive in dealing with the natural environment. Once the forms in which American power was organized produced such prodigies of good things–wealth, entertainment, education, security and prestige among the nations–that all questions seemed foolish and the future was assured. But now the signs of powerlessness are everywhere: in our inability either to pulverize a small Asian nation or to withdraw our armies from it; in the breakdown of administrative structures designed to provide such basic services as welfare, education, medical care, public transportation, electricity, mail, and law enforcement; in the deepening realization that our attempt to organize human life in an urban form has probably failed; in the helplessness and growing anger over racial and minority problems where each solution only exposes deeper complexities; and in the despairing discovery that we have perfected a technological dynamic too powerful and depleting for the environment in which we live.

One consequence of our growing sense of powerlessness is a loss of confidence in the efficacy of our political institutions and ideals. It is a commonplace among academic analysts of American politics that the effective operation of the system depends on small elites rather than on popular participation. Although the fact that the system has endured at all is a constant source of wonder and delight to political scientists, most of them are certain that if efforts were made to democratize it, the system would founder in weakness and irrationality. Equally significantly, most of the recent studies of the American voter have underscored the presence of precisely those reactions and attitudes which reflect the state of society; its powerlessness mirrors their apathy, despair, and impotence. It is one of the curiosities of contemporary social science that feelings of powerlessness are still interpreted to be characteristic of "the authoritarian personality." Given the realities of technological society, such feelings are more like an affirmation of sanity.

The most common example of the paradox that the American political system has become more and more powerful and increasingly less effective is the institution of the Presidency. Since the New Deal there has been a great increase in Presidential power, especially over foreign relations and the armed forces. Yet the constant complaint of both students and incumbents of the office is that the President has become progressively helpless in controlling his swollen staff, absorbing the daily flood of information, and planning and acting for the future. Thus the paradox of an institution which has grown to gargantuan size and yet is periodically threatened by weakness and confusion, as the decision to invade Cambodia so clearly showed. In retrospect, it was not only the decision itself that was disturbing but also the fact that it was taken amid administrative chaos and near breakdown.

The most telling cases of the powerlessness produced by power are found in foreign and military policy. Following World War II, American influence and presence throughout the world formed an extraordinary extension of our advanced technology and weaponry. But beginning with the Korean War the record changes: two wars against small nations but no victories; the catastrophe of the Bay of Pigs and the near nuclear disaster of the Cuban missile crisis; a running crisis in the Middle East while we are so badly exposed in Vietnam.

The paradox of powerless power was revealed in a phrase which the President repeated in announcing the Cambodian invasion: we must show the world, he said, that we are not "an impotent giant." The temptation of a giant stung by tiny enemies is to summon greater powers, in this case, perhaps, tactical nuclear weapons–just as he is tempted to employ the shocking weapons of increased surveillance, preventive detention, and severe police measures in the "war against crime," against the "bums" on the campuses, and all the other nagging domestic problems. Frustration, in its self-destructiveness, has also brought the President and some congressmen to turn their rage against the Supreme Court, the one institution which has attempted to stay abreast of its responsibilities, even at the cost of shouldering burdens dodged by President and Congress in such areas as civil rights, draft laws, and criminal procedures.

The deepening perplexities of American society were reflected on the campuses during the Sixties in a special way. The typically critical attitudes of the young and many intellectuals turned first into skepticism toward the professed virtues of American culture and institutions, and then grew into profound revulsion against the main values and organizations which sustained the American quest for power. A restless search for new values and new modes of action began. At the same time, the campuses shared with the rest of society the growing sense of collective and individual impotence.

There is no need to document again the growing rejection among the young of the values and life styles of corporate, technological, and imperial America. Similarly, it is superfluous to recite how technological society seems to the young to offer little in the way of meaningful work. They see the system as a vast processing plant which converts human lives into trash for consumption and weapons for destruction. The rejection of society has been accompanied by an equally profound hostility to the education designed to serve society's ends.

This has meant not only a turn against the technical disciplines—thereby renouncing the power and vocational security which they offer—but also a revolt against many of the standard liberal academic subjects and methods of teaching, on the ground that they encourage powerlessness and irrelevance. There is something like a romantic revolt against both technical and liberal knowledge going on on the campuses, a yearning to break through what Blake called "single vision," a superficial Kierkegaardian conviction that "subjectivity, inwardness is truth." Most of the values associated with the liberal and humanistic studies seem either incomprehensible or soporific: what does it mean any longer to work, to become a person, to strive to fulfill one's potentialities, or to take seriously any of the other traditional exhortations of liberal education? The promise of liberal education—that it was possible to unite vocation with moral growth, success with social contribution, production with beauty—seems so much chaff spread by desiccated dons unaware that the academy is a desert or a disaster area.

The sense of futility which pervades the campuses can also be understood as an expression of the plight of the middle classes today. Historically, the middle classes shaped their identity in demanding the release of human energy. All of the great bourgeois revolutions sought to liberate individual power from the restraints of custom, inherited status, and religious and intellectual authority. Mobility, opportunity, and progress were the watchwords of a class bent on moving upward and outward. Classical middle-class liberalism not only trumpeted the cause of freedom and property but, as writers like J. S. Mill and John Dewey made clear, it extolled fluidity and growth as prime desiderata in the culture of society.

Much of this outlook persisted into the mid-twentieth century, but it is now on the wane. It is not surprising that the centers of the student revolt have been the campuses which most faithfully reflected middle-class values and aspirations or that the children of the middle class should have supplied the cadres of revolt. Since technological society is the supreme achievement of the middle class, the appearance of crisis will fall hardest on the progeny of the middle class. The crisis of such a society does not take the form of severe economic depression or widespread feelings of exploitation or injustice. These phenomena do exist in some measure but they are largely restricted to minority groups whose minorityness is fixed and incapable of expansion. Instead crisis develops when the pains and discontents of powerlessness outweigh the values and rewards of powerfulness.

The affluence of technological society persists through the crisis because the crisis is not, fundamentally, one of production or distribution. The crisis is spiritual and psychic rather than material. Its prophets are Blake rather than Marx, James rather than Dewey.

Much of the novel activity on the campuses expresses a quest for new forms of power by those who feel themselves powerless. Some of these new forms of power are cultural rather than political. Dress, language, music, and drugs become weapons of mockery and provocation, not only *pour épater les bourgeois*, but to claim authority and exert influence. Other forms, more properly political, have also been invented or adapted: mass rallies, sit-ins, student strikes, disruption, and violence. The politicization of the campuses thus appears as an expression of powerlessness; and politics, along with the cultural revolution, becomes a way of claiming legitimacy and demanding change. The pervasiveness of politics corresponds to the widening of the crisis itself, while the intensity with which political and cultural power is being pursued by the young is a measure of their despair and powerlessness.

The last step in this "theory" concerns the choice of a word. What is the appropriate general term for describing the campus events of the last six years?

Various words of varying intensity have been used to describe the events: disturbances, unrest, troubles, rebellion, revolution. Of these, the most intense is revolution. Even though writers in our time have trivialized the term by applying it to everything from rising hemlines to landings on the moon, it remains one of the most serious political words, freighted with heavy historical associations, readying its user for extreme attitudes and actions.

Is revolution an appropriate word for the events which have occurred on the campuses?

The assumption which underlies these essays is that while the profound changes in the attitudes, values, and behavior of many young people perhaps amount to a cultural revolution, they are far from being a political revolution. Certainly there have been important changes: many are discussed in one or another of the essays and we shall attempt an assessment of the most important ones in the *Epilogue*. But revolution has to do with fundamental transformations. And not all transformations are fundamental, just as not all fundamental transformations are political. On the political side, what has taken place on the campuses is best described as rebellion against the established forms and holders of authority and search for new modes of authority.

Many students and some faculty have challenged the policies and rules governing their campuses and refused to comply with them. The refusal has occasionally taken violent forms. The lack of respect for campus rules and officials is a part of the "delegitimization" of authority that generally pervades our culture. But, while respect for authority has declined because of what students have refused to offer to it, its forms and grounds remain intact. The students have refused authority its proper reverence, but they have not seized much, if any, of its vital substance, power.

Take the demand for "student power" for example. It was one of the genuine innovations of the period, and some of the doctrine and rhetoric that accompanied it had a revolutionary thrust. But in practice, its impact has been reformist and conservative. Students have achieved a modest voice on judicial, administrative, and deliberative bodies on a good many campuses. Changes of this kind are entirely consistent with the democratic values and the "ethic of responsibility" which higher education is supposed to promote. After the initial distress, such changes have been welcomed by those who worried much about students' unwillingness to "work within the system" and play by "the rules of the game." Moreover, despite a few bizarre course proposals, students have shown about as much curricular inventiveness and political passion as the professors and administrators they have joined. Finally, student participation has been pretty thoroughly contained within the standard forms of academic governance and held short of the ultimate questions. To our knowledge student power nowhere affects significantly—let alone determines—the selection of college presidents, trustees, and faculty. And no campus in the land has been transformed into a participatory democracy where the community is summoned by a blast from Piggy's conch.

So much for the general context of assumptions within which the essays were written. We shall return to some of these themes in the *Epilogue*.

I
Berkeley and the Fate of the Multiversity

This first essay treats the Berkeley beginnings of the campus revolt. The events and situations described here constituted the heroic age of a movement which, as it dragged on at Berkeley and spread to other campuses, became more ambiguous.

In that long past fall of 1964, the issues were relatively simple. They were the classically libertarian ones of free speech, political rights, and due process. The Vietnam war and the draft hardly figured at all. Lines were clearly drawn between students and Administration, with the faculty gradually moving to the support of the students but retaining its corporate independence and influence. The governing body of the entire university system, the Board of Regents, was ineffectual rather than vicious. University President Clark Kerr, one of the most impressive figures in the recent history of American higher education, retained and, on the whole, ably exercised actual control of the system. Although the voters soon grew indignant and resentful toward the student rebels and their faculty allies, the official political climate remained that of the mild liberalism of Governor Pat Brown and Assemblyman Jesse Unruh.

Doubtless the reader will be struck by the innocence and idealism of most of the youthful actors–and by the hopeful tone of the essay itself. The rhetoric and temper of the students were unideological, trusting, and non-violent. Their tactics, while new to the campus, had deep roots in the civil rights movement. It was a time of splendid political speech and skillful political action. The student rebels and the faculty majority clearly thought they had won a notable and enduring victory. The only portent of trouble ahead was the growing acceptance in high administrative and political quarters of a conspiracy theory of the uprising. As the suspicion grew that the campus would not return to the peaceful status quo ante, *so too grew the temptation to blame the troubles on a handful of student militants and outside agitators. To accept the alternative view, that disaffection was pervasive, would open questions that would go to the heart of the system itself.*

MARCH 11, 1965

It isn't often that a great university suddenly goes smash, yet this is what happened to the Berkeley campus during the first week of December, 1964. During that week the University of California (Berkeley), numbering 27,000 students, 12,000 faculty and non-academic employees, numerous research laboratories, institutes, old-fashioned classrooms and boasting an annual budget of $60 million, suffered an almost total collapse. Campus authority vanished, academic routines were reduced to a shambles, and the prophecy of Mario Savio was fulfilled: the "machine" came to a "grinding halt."

This brought to a climax a succession of events, each more astonishing than the one before, which had kept the University in a continuous ferment since mid-September.

It is no surprise that those outside the University community have been unable to make sense of these events, for even the participants themselves often had trouble in understanding their own behavior. Many of the student demands and tactics seemed outlandish and more appropriate to Birmingham than to Berkeley. The responses of University officials wavered between treating the student movement as a Children's Crusade, a Communist conspiracy, and "a civil rights panty raid" (as one administrator saw it). The most outlandish behavior, however, came neither from the students nor the myopic deans, but from those specifically charged with governing the institution. Supporting the seemingly invulnerable institution in its moment of crisis was a broad array of interested and powerful elements: the Governor and Board of Regents; interest groups which had long prospered from the services and needs of the University; and a suspicious and hostile public, misled by the local press into believing that agitators were destroying the University and moved by an urge to punish the young for their seeming lack of gratitude for all the advantages which a generous citizenry had given them. Yet the authority of the University crumpled under the pressure of a few thousand students who had no other power than the moral courage to say "no" before the colossus and the tactical skill to say it at the right time and in unison.

Absurd it may have been, but it was not trivial. The events destroyed some illusions about contemporary education and disclosed the depths of the antagonism between a generation which has all but contracted out of the affluent society and the perfect dehumanized expression of that society, the large-scale organization, which transmutes knowledge, energy, and money into technological miracles—the perfect artifact for multiplying change so as to drown out purpose. In a society which values growth and material power above all else, and which cannot comprehend why rebellion and discontent should flourish amid plenty and opportunity, it was astonishing to observe the students making a moral protest in defense of traditional rights which their elders could not take seriously and in defense of the principles of a liberal education which their elders had mislaid somewhere among the many other functions of the "multiversity." The crisis demonstrated that socially useful functions, no matter how competently performed, are no substitute for moral authority.

Had the students not succeeded in creating an instrument to convert their moral outrage into power, their protests would have died unheard. The Free Speech Movement came into existence during the first week in October, and from then on it enjoyed a near monopoly on the expression of protest. It attracted widespread support and enlisted the energies of thousands of students for the numerous tasks demanded by a political struggle. Although its wide support gave it a heterogeneous quality—stretching from the radical right to the radical left—its political style was uniquely expressive of the new generation. It was highly conscious of political and social issues; its language was radical and its tactics aggressive, but pervaded by a novel blend of moralism and impudence ("liberal" and "fink" were almost synonymous, "textbook" was made to sound like "pornography"). There is no doubt that there were devious motives among its leaders; that occasionally they became intoxicated by their sudden power and made noises as if they intended to smash the whole system; that here and there extreme leftists were to be found. Yet it would be a serious mistake to suggest, as other writers have, that the entire crisis was fabricated and dominated by subversives or riffraff. It has been well established that most of the followers were intelligent students who were novices in political action. The sacrifices of many who were willing to place their careers on the line, the spontaneity of their indignation, the warm fellowship of their movement, and their unfailing good humor were too real to be explained by subterranean conspiracies. Those who believe that, by definition, a problem does not exist if it can be shown that radicals are somehow involved are not about to acknowledge the dominating idealism of the movement. At bottom the unbelievers must fear that the situation is really worse than even the conspiracy theory suggests: if it is possible for so many–faculty and students alike–to be duped by so few, then the condition of one of the world's greatest universities is more hopeless than even its critics charge.

The many issues raised during these chaotic months can be classified under two broad headings. First, there were political and constitutional issues centering around whether the University should place any but the most minimal restrictions upon the exercise of political rights by students on campus, and whether the University should restrain and discipline political acts or advocacy performed on the campus but leading to illegal acts off the campus (e.g., a political rally called on campus to organize an illegal sit-in at a hotel). Historically, the Administration had based its highly restrictive policies on a provision of the state constitution requiring that "the University shall be entirely independent of all political or sectarian influence and kept free therefrom in the appointment of its Regents and in the administration of its affairs." This became the justification for prohibiting political advocacy and activity on campus, for defining what activities were political, and for denying the use of campus facilities for organizing off-campus political actions. The policy of the Administration was determined primarily by the desire to prevent the involvement of the University in public controversy.

The students' general contention was that they should have the same political rights on campus that they enjoyed as citizens off the campus, and that determinations of the legality of off-campus actions should be reserved exclusively to the courts. In addition, the students argued that the constitutional provision upon which the Administration relied was intended to prevent the University itself from becoming involved in politics, and to prevent the governors of the University from applying political criteria in the conduct of University affairs, but was not intended to deny students the right to engage in political action not involving the name of the University. Finally, the students argued that the Administration had been highly arbitrary in the day-to-day application of its rules.

An overwhelming majority of the faculty was gradually persuaded that the student argument was generally correct. As early as October 13 the faculty had affirmed its support for "maximum freedom for student political activity" and on December 8 formally resolved that there should be only minimal regulations on the *form* of political speech and action on campus, no University controls on the *content* of expression, and no University sanctions on the off-campus political activities of its students.

The second broad range of issues related to the

University itself. The gross size and population of the campus, the numerous research and service functions carried on, its intimate connections with outside interests have transformed the old categories of "teacher" and "academic community" into "researcher" and "multiversity" or "knowledge factory" (the last phrases are those of its president). Unlike many private institutions, Berkeley's character was not established by a founder or given shape by a religious sect determined to bring piety and learning to a rude society. Ungraced by traditions, its graduates lack a distinctive stamp. Above all, identities are hard to come by and definitions difficult to pronounce when an institution is determined to gear its life and growth to the needs of an ever-expanding society, or at least to the needs of society's most powerful and clamorous parts. In *The Uses of the University*, President Clark Kerr writes that the multiversity has "no prophet to proclaim its vision; no guardian to protect its sanctity." The clear implication is that the multiversity dare not risk self-definition. It must remain "as confused as possible for the sake of the preservation of the whole uneasy balance" among the interests and pressures that make up its environment. If it is the multiversity's nature not to have a nature, there is comfort in knowing that it is "an imperative . . . rooted in the logic of history." The beauty of an imperative is that it provides a "justification" for virtually anything, including the mish-mash of activities that have found a home in the multiversity.

Kerr's realization that the condition of the multiversity's existence is also the source of its weakness imports an element of desperation into his analysis. His use of industrial metaphors disguises the inherent anarchy of the multiversity system. There is a touch of melancholy in his conclusion that "the task is to keep this lawlessness within reasonable bounds." In the end the university is reduced to being a puppet, twitching to stimuli it cannot control, powerless to set its own direction. "The process cannot be stopped. The results cannot be foreseen. It remains to adapt."

If one is startled by this confession of drift by the head of the enterprise, how much more unprepared one is for his cynicism. The university is characterized as "a mechanism held together by administrative rules and powered by money." The faculty is "a series of individual . . . entrepreneurs held together by a common grievance over parking." For all their sprightliness, these epigrams sag–melancholy testimony that the realist is second to none in his illusions. Their author is the same man who early in the crisis denied that a "freedom of speech issue" existed and who, after the faculty voted overwhelmingly to eliminate restrictions on the content of expression, demeaned the motives of that distinguished body by attributing its action to petty jealousy toward the other campuses in the system.

An examination of the pattern of events at Berkeley shows how great is the distance and how difficult the communication between those who make the multiversity's rules and those who must live by them.

The controversy opened on an appropriate note. On September 14, the Administration blandly announced that a narrow strip of land at the entrance to the campus was really University property and not, as previously assumed, the property of the city (uncertain as to its own identity the multiversity has never been sure where it ends and the world begins). This strip had been the locus of student political activity. Since it was assumed to lie outside the campus, University regulations restricting political activity did not apply. Without consulting the students, the Administration closed off the main outlet for political energies, claiming at first that these activities interfered with pedestrian traffic, but later reaffirming its position that "University facilities may not, of course, be used to support or advocate off-campus political or social action."

The students immediately formed a united front, ranging from Goldwaterites to Socialists, to urge the restoration of a free speech area and the modification of the rules. The Chancellor then issued a "clarification," the first of a long series that came to follow a familiar pattern of concession and contradiction, giving an over-all impression of weakness. The students were allowed to use the steps of the administration building, Sproul Hall, as a free speech area and to man tables on "the strip," but not for political purposes. The students proceeded to ignore this last restriction, and the Administration to ignore the violations. Tables were set up and political speeches given in forbidden areas. Again the Chancellor gave ground and permitted students to support candidates in the November elections and to take stands on state propositions. This gave something to everybody: the students might oppose an amendment repealing the state fair housing law, while the University could continue its efforts for an educational bond issue. Characteristically, the Chancellor followed these concessions with a show of firmness which he then undercut by his own actions. He stated on September 28 that the matter was "closed," but then had his deans select eight students, including three leaders, from among hundreds who claimed to have violated the regulations. The eight were suspended "indefinitely"—a penalty unknown to University rules.

This led to the first great blowup: On October 1 a large rally formed in front of Sproul Hall. A police car taking to jail a person charged with manning a table unlawfully was surrounded and stranded in a sea of students. Mario Savio, considerately barefoot, mounted the car and harangued the crowd. Two hundred students then entered Sproul for a sit-in. Faculty efforts at mediation were blocked by the Chancellor's stubborn insistence that regulations and disciplinary measures were not negotiable. As the tension continued into the next day, a faculty group by-passed the Chancellor and persuaded President Kerr of the need for compromise. This began the gradual eclipse of the Chancellor by the President, thus underscoring the fact that each campus of the multiversity lacks autonomy and is headed only by an expendable functionary, suitably called "the chief campus officer." An agreement was reached with Kerr, but not before he had summoned 500 police and threatened to have them disperse the crowd unless an agreement was reached. The students agreed to halt the demonstrations and in return the University agreed to restore the privileges of certain suspended groups, to submit the cases of the eight to a committee of the Academic Senate, to drop its charges against the man encapsulated in the police car, and to establish a committee of faculty, students, and administrators to study the rules.

The agreement was a disaster. Neither the Administration nor students acquitted themselves with honor. The Chancellor appointed ten of the twelve members of the tripartite committee without seeking recommendations from either students or faculty. He also assigned the cases of the eight to a committee of his own choosing, not to one appointed by the Academic Senate. In response to protests, Kerr again intervened to retrieve the situation. The cases of the eight were transferred to a committee established by the Senate. This committee, after hearings, recommended that six of the students be reinstated immediately. A six-week suspension was recommended for the other two. The committee's report was also highly critical of the Administration's procedures. The Chancellor announced that he would not respond to these recommendations until the following month.

Meanwhile, the tripartite committee foundered. The truculence of the FSM representatives, combined with the refusal of the Administration's spokesmen to surrender disciplinary powers over "illegal" advocacy, created an impasse. The FSM resumed the manning of tables. The Chancellor then dissolved the tripartite committee on the grounds that the students had violated the agreement of October 2. From November 9 to November 20, the students continued to violate the regulations while the Administration enforced them selectively, now citing seventy students for infractions, now ignoring massive violations.

On November 20 the Board of Regents, highest authority in the entire university system, met. The Board is wondrously representative of the genius of the multiversity. It would be difficult to design a more attractive target for students nurtured on the C. Wright Mills doctrine of the conservative power elite. It is composed mainly of high politicians, wealthy financiers, industrialists and businessmen, and the remarkable Max Rafferty. Kerr persuaded the Board to overturn its prohibition against all on-campus political activity and advocacy, although the ban against "illegal advocacy" was retained. The Board's *quid pro quo* was a recommendation that students who had violated the rules during the past three months should be disciplined. It also dealt with the cases of the eight students and recommended reinstatement of the whole group but refused to expunge the charges against them.

The Regents nearly restored peace. The FSM was badly split; a sit-in in Sproul on November 23 was called off after a few hours, indicating that the remaining area of controversy was too limited to be inflammatory. Just when most faculty and students were resuming normal routines, the Chancellor restored chaos by a master stroke of stupidity, bad timing, and injustice. He sent letters to four students, including three top leaders of FSM, informing them that the University intended to bring charges for actions committed eight weeks earlier. By reopening a matter which everyone had assumed to be closed, he, with one blow, revived FSM, outraged the faculty, and focused the question in its starkest terms: how is it possible to justify an authority so grossly insensitive to the spirit of an academic institution?

Two days later, on December 2, nearly 800 students filed into Sproul Hall for the climactic sit-in. The next day Governor Brown called in 600 police to clear the students from the building and hustle them off to jail. The faculty rallied to the students: cars were provided to return them from jail and a bail fund was set up and quickly oversubscribed. While all this was going on, the graduate students had organized a strike which successfully halted most classes for two days. The students had fulfilled their vow: the machine was stopped.

Up to this point, the faculty as a body had remained relatively detached, though a few individuals had occasionally been involved in the controversy. But now the collapse of authority and the sight of nearly 600 armed policemen shocked the faculty into the recognition that it alone was left to pick up the pieces. For a time, the faculty forgot its lust for research, its shameful neglect of teaching, its acquiescence in the bureaucratization of the University. Setting aside the ethos of power and growth, the faculty stirred to ancestral memories of the ideal of a community of scholars bound together in the spirit of friendly persuasion and pledged to truth rather than abundance. It had been clear all along that while the students' protests were directed against the Administration, their entreaties were directed to the faculty, but it took a shattering experience to restore the faculty memories of fellowship with the students. Now that its collective conscience was awakened, the faculty found the energy and vision necessary for the task of reconstruction. A few writers have attributed subsequent faculty action to hysteria. It is puzzling why men should find it necessary to deny the faculty its finest hour and to equate decisiveness with panic, moral impulse with fear.

One line of faculty action was in response to the impotence of the Chancellor whose withdrawal and increasing isolation left the campus leaderless. A committee of departmental chairmen was formed to impress upon the President the gravity of the situation. After exhausting negotiations, the chairmen wrung from the President and a group of Regents a promise not to add University punishment to court sentences of the sit-ins. It is symbolic that the chairmen's group and the Regents never talked face-to-face. University rules forbid faculty members from making direct approaches to the Regents; hence the two parties were closeted in separate rooms of an airport motel and the President plied between them.

The amnesty was a necessary precondition for resolving the crisis, but the Kerr-Chairmen Agreement was silent on the fundamental questions of political freedom which the students had been raising. That silence provoked outbursts of protest when the President and a distinguished faculty member presented the terms of the armistice to the campus community assembled in the Greek Theater. Moreover, their rhetoric of affluence and order revealed a fatal ignorance of the yearnings and commitments of the present generation of students. ("Today we decide whether we shall move ahead productively and in peace. . . . This community has been divided not so much on ends as on means. . . . We must seek added funds. . . . We must face external investigations. . . . We must face . . . a transition from the extensive growth of the past century to the intensive growth of the indefinite future—for growth must never stop.")

The second line of faculty action proved more successful. It led directly to the resolutions of December 8 which asserted that the rights demanded by the students could not be denied by a university. Moreover, it created the first stirrings of a faculty attempt to reform the multiversity. The success of this second attack grew out of a fusion of discontent and shame. That a university had resorted to force against its students seemed an absolute confirmation of the ineptitude and moral bankruptcy of the system. It was widely believed, therefore, that the Chancellor must go. Also fresh in the minds of the faculty were the recent and shameful handling of a case involving academic freedom and the arbitrary decision to revise the entire pattern of University life ("year-round operation" of "the plant," the President described it).

Throughout November several groups of faculty members had been formulating proposals to meet the problem of student political activities, but the events of December 2 generated the passion necessary to unite the faculty. On December 4 an impromptu faculty meeting was called and the discussion there disclosed a deep sentiment among the vast majority for policies that would set no limits upon the *content* of expression and only such minimal restraints upon the *forms* of expression as were necessary to the performance of ordinary University functions. The faculty was also becoming persuaded that the intricate legal questions surrounding "illegal" speech and "conspiracy" were not the proper business of any university authority.

On December 8 these sentiments, now refined in the form of resolutions, were brought before the Academic Senate and passed by a vote of 824 to 115. The resolutions provided that: (1) only the "time, place, and manner" of on-campus political activity should be regulated to "prevent interference with the normal functions of the University"; (2) the content of speech was not to be restricted; (3) off-campus political activities should not be subject to University regulations; (4) disciplinary questions arising out of the minimal regulations in (1) should be handled by a faculty committee, i.e., the Administration was not to touch such matters.

Two additional resolutions were passed. One created an Emergency Executive Committee to act for the faculty in further matters arising out of the crisis, and the other called for a committee to study the question of how the faculty might make itself more effective in the general governance of the University. The importance of these changes was quickly demonstrated, for the next encounter took place elsewhere, at the December 18 meeting of the Board of Regents.

The Regents have final power in almost every area of University affairs. Usually their meetings deal with ordinary matters of University business, but this was to be no ordinary meeting. More like a summit conference, it was surrounded by an atmosphere of urgency and intense public concern. What occurred is not easy to reconstruct because part of the meeting was secret; what was decided is not entirely clear because of the muddled language of the public statement issued later. It seems that the Regents have finally recognized the First and Fourteenth Amendments, and that henceforth students will be allowed maximum political freedom on the campus. It is clear that students may now use campus facilities for organizing off-campus actions. However, the Regents continued to balk at the use of campus facilities for mounting illegal off-campus actions, and hence reserved authority to discipline students in such matters. The Regents also refused to devolve upon the faculty final authority over student disciplinary cases in political questions.

Despite the face-saving vagueness of their formulations, the Regents had come far since September. Their allusion to the First and Fourteenth Amendments was a tacit confession that most University rules affecting speech and action were unconstitutional, and their decision not to punish the arrested students raised the hope that eventually they would relinquish jurisdiction over cases where off-campus actions turn out to be illegal. Moreover, in announcing their willingness to consult with students and faculty to improve campus rules, the Regents recognized what the faculty had sensed earlier: students must be viewed as participating members of the academic community.

This summary of the Regents' action does not convey the fact that bloody fighting took place behind the scenes. There is little doubt that Kerr had persuaded the Regents to accept the broad direction of the faculty proposals and to leave undisturbed the amnesty agreement of December 7. It is equally clear that the Chancellor had fought for his life by taking a "hard line" on both the question of rules and amnesty. He lost and shortly thereafter was replaced by a new acting chancellor. Once again Kerr had demonstrated his extraordinary political abilities. He had averted a calamitous showdown by persuading the Regents to alter the rules, but he had also neutralized to some degree the bid for autonomy implicit in the Berkeley resolutions. This he accomplished by his time-honored tactic of employing the machinery of the state-wide system, and the envies of Berkeley represented in it, to condemn local solutions and quell assertions of local autonomy. He acquiesced to the fact that Berkeley's chancellor had lost all credit, but later, when it became apparent that the new chancellor was attracting growing enthusiasm, Kerr gratuitously reminded the campus that the old chancellor was "just tired and wanted to get away," but that he would "most likely" return.

As matters now stand, the faculty and students have gained most of the objectives contained in the December 8 resolutions. Assuming that good sense prevails among the parties, that the few zealots in the legislature do not persist in their announced aim of firing masses of students and faculty, and that the impending trial of the sit-ins does not reopen old wounds, the prospects for honorable peace are good. But peace is not necessarily the same as normality, for the events of the first semester cut too deep to permit a restoration of the old ways. A university is in the process of being redefined. Its president has recently proclaimed that "the primary responsibility of the university is the education of its students. A second major responsibility is research . . ." (a draft of the University's ten-year program made last fall had no mention of "primary" emphasis upon education). But the basic element in all redefinitions is the new breed of students who have appeared on the Berkeley campus.

Published accounts of the student movement have radically distorted its character. Some of these accounts have been almost delusional in quality. There is, for example, Professor Lewis Feuer's denial that there were any genuine issues at stake and his claim that very few genuine students were involved in the controversy. He attributes the uprising to the powers of a handful of crackpots, political extremists, drug addicts, and sexual libertines—most of them, thank God, not students at all, but spoiled personalities, tormented members of that underground Berkeley community of *lumpen*-intellectuals—who managed to dupe thousands of innocent and true students into believing that there were real issues, thereby capturing the ever-present hostility of the young against their elders and mobilizing it into a "generational uprising." Less imaginative men than Feuer have characterized the movement as the subversive work of leftist plotters. In this view, the campus will not find peace until it surgically removes these diseased members from the student body politic.

Another way to avoid the challenge of understanding is to concentrate all attention upon one aspect of the reality, and then to interpret that reality in very narrow categories. Specifically, this approach characterizes the behavior and tactics of the students as riotous and irresponsible, and condemns them as illegal, thereby foreclosing the issues. Some of the students' actions were illegal, but that still leaves open the questions of whether they were necessary and morally justified. Furthermore, and contrary to the impression spread by the mass media, the students were not tempestuous and violent. With few exceptions, they behaved with dignity and restraint.

All of these accounts dissolve the real problem into a vapor of fantasies congenial to the commentator. None of them recognizes that there were real students asserting real grievances within an institutional setting that had in fact become pathological. As President Kerr himself noted, the students have been "restless" for some time. An adequate account must take a serious look at the sources of that restlessness.

For some time now, the students, especially the undergraduates, have felt themselves to be an alien presence within the multiversity, an "Other Academia" analogous to the "Other America," ill-fed, ill-housed, and ill-clothed not in the material sense but in the intellectual and spiritual senses. As the multiversity has climbed to higher and higher peaks of research productivity, material riches, and bureaucratic complexity, the students have fallen into deeper and deeper abysses of hostility and estrangement. The students' own favorite word for their condition is "alienation," by which they mean a number of things, and especially a sense of not being valued members of a genuine intellectual and moral community. Their feeling is grounded in reality.

The architects of the multiversity simply have not solved the problem of how to build an institution which not only produces knowledge and knowledgeable people with useful skills, but which also enriches and enlightens the lives of its students—informing them with the values of the intellect, preparing them to serve as the guardians of society's intellectual honesty and political health, arming them with the vision by which society seeks its own better future. It is the performance of these latter tasks that distinguishes a genuine educational community from a mere research factory and training institution. Hence, as Harold Taylor has said, "The mark of a true university is whether or not it takes its students seriously."

By any reasonable standard, the multiversity has not taken its students seriously. At Berkeley, the educational environment of the undergraduate is bleak. He is confronted throughout his entire first two years with indifferent advising, endless bureaucratic routines, gigantic lecture courses, and a deadening succession of textbook assignments and bluebook examinations testing his grasp of bits and pieces of knowledge. All too often the difference between the last two years of a student's education and the first two is chronological rather than qualitative. It is possible to take a B.A. at Berkeley and never talk with a professor. To many of the students, the whole system seems a perversion of an educational community into a factory designed for the mass processing of men into machines. The image is a bit excessive, to be sure, but like any good caricature this one distorts reality in order to clarify it. A great many faculty members have acknowledged the essential justice of the students' case against the multiversity, and have confessed their own not-so-small contribution to the malaise. Faculty conversation at Berkeley is now haunted by remorseful allusions to the bleak realities of student life.

The reality seems all the bleaker by contrast with the glowing expectations which students are now bringing to the university. Young people today are conditioned from the earliest age to see "education" as the magic key to all the delectable things. They come to college in search, not merely of knowledge, but of salvation. College is the real thing, they are told, and when the real thing turns out to look a lot like the sham they left behind, they are understandably distressed.

It costs relatively little money to attend the University of California, but unlike most other state universities, California has high admission standards. The freshman class is selected from the top 10 percent of high-school seniors. This means that not only are the students of high average intelligence, but that they also have worked hard and kept "clean" throughout their high-school years. Furthermore, Cal students, like all others, bring with them to college youth's natural exuberance, but relatively little of this energy is drained off through the customary and "safe" channels of sports, organized social life, and seasonal bacchanals. Most of the energy finds other outlets.

Most of the students live in private accommodations, and their private lives do seem quite experimental and free—though not as orgiastic as the fevered imaginations of some professors and deans would suggest. More importantly, over the past decade the students have become increasingly serious—about themselves, their studies, and their society. But there is still a lot of energy left, and at Berkeley, unlike most other American colleges, a good bit of this is poured into political and social causes. For example, Berkeley in particular, and the San Francisco Bay Area in general, have sent more young people to the South in the struggle for racial justice than any other place except New York. The word has gone out: things are happening at Berkeley. The events of last semester, with all the publicity they gained, will increase this magnetic attraction—a thought horrifying enough to bring a dean to consider resigning his post.

Beyond the immediate attractions of a lively campus, many students today, especially those in the humanities and social sciences, are aware of the shortcomings of their society and are passionately looking for authentic values to replace what they perceive as the phony slogans and spiritual tawdriness of so much of the public rhetoric and action of our time. Few of them come to college with an ideology, nor do they seek one while there. Rather, theirs is an ethic of sincerity and personal encounter. They take ideals seriously and are quick to detect evasion, posturing, and double-think. If their conception of the educational process is somewhat romantic and woolly—tending to equate the exchange of impressions and sentiments with learning, impatient with discipline, and inclined to rush off after a dozen exciting novelties at once—it is still more attractive than the emphasis on utility and training favored in the multiversity establishment. The latter is a bleakness of spirit, closed and immobile; while the former is a plenitude of spirit, open and vital. Such students constitute a university's most valuable resource, and it is a delight and a privilege to teach them. There were a great many such students, graduate as well as undergraduate, involved in the happenings at Berkeley. Given all the loose talk about student "riots" and "radicals," it is necessary to emphasize this point.

There were radicals among the leadership of the FSM, but there is no evidence to indicate that the movement's leaders were the slaves of ideologies that blinded them to reality, or led them into attempts to subvert the true purposes of their mass following–which, to say it again, were freedom of political expression and educational reform. Furthermore, the vast majority of the students shared the goals of the FSM, and a near majority also supported their direct-action tactics. The "radicalism" of this mass following consisted in little more than devotion to some traditional principles which their elders had taught them, plus that impatience with the conservatism of the old which the young ought to have. Radical ideology, then, mattered little in the events at Berkeley. What mattered far more was a clear-eyed and courageous response to concrete, felt injustices.

There were no riots. Save for the incident of the "captured" police car, the mass rallies, sit-ins, and the student strike were all conducted with admirable dignity and calm. There were a few scattered episodes of excessive behavior by individuals under extreme stress. There were many intemperate words. Many University rules and a few state laws were broken.

All of this is regrettable, but understandable, and not unjustifiable. These students were acting in a situation where, time and again, officials refused to listen to them, behaved whimsically and punitively, and altogether gave the impression that the student cause was without justice. The students responded with the only methods that could make the Administration listen, and many of them showed a clearer appreciation than their elders of the moral burdens involved in the use of pressure tactics within an academic setting. What happened at Berkeley cannot be understood as the delinquent outbursts of fanatics and ungrateful rebels. These students broke the rules and the law in an agonizing effort to compel an Administration which, by its unwillingness to listen to their just claims and to treat them as participating members of a community of the intellect, inevitably brought about its own moral downfall and forfeited its claim to willing obedience. To many of the students, such conduct left no alternative but direct action.

The events of the past semester have not cast a foreboding shadow over the future of education at Berkeley. It is clear to many of us here that the students reminded us of some basic values that were disappearing in the thoughtless rush for the future. Very much of what they did had to be done before anyone would listen. The result is, at this moment, a climate of respect and concern that offers more promise than has been present in a long time that the future of this university can be a noble one.

II
The University Revolution

This essay registered the changes which had taken place in Berkeley in the two years since 1964. The apparent victory of 1964 had been hollowed out, and hope had turned sour. The quality of student leadership had declined, and the Regents were in a strident and vengeful mood. Vietnam and the draft had become major issues. Although the student movement was fragmented and querulous, some unity was provided by a vague but pervasive ideology composed largely of vulgar Marxism, the populism of C. Wright Mills, and elements of hip culture. From the meeting of the two cultures, political and hip, a new politics began to emerge, new in style, language, rhythm, and tactics. The slogan of student power was prominent for the first time.

*But the main significance of the period from January, 1965, to January, 1967, was the failure of the Berkeley faculty and Administration to seize the opportunity and deal boldly with the challenges of educational reform and student participation. The momentum generated by the FSM, together with the idealism, good will, and hope which accompanied it, could have been directed toward fundamental and much needed changes. Moreover, in the Muscatine Report (*Education at Berkeley, *March, 1966) and in another report (*The Culture of the University:

Governance and Education, *1968), the campus was presented with far-reaching proposals for educational and constitutional reform.*

The faculty responded to the Muscatine Report by accepting its smallest proposals and ignoring the major ones. The Governance Report was totally rejected by both faculty and Administration. Ironically, this report was to have considerable influence on other campuses where the issues of student participation were approached in a more constructive way. Events at Berkeley soon demonstrated the high costs of these missed opportunities, just as they showed the end results of the logic of law and order which had come to dominate not only the campus faculty and Administration but, with the inauguration of Governor Reagan in January of 1967, the political climate of the state as well.

This essay also explores some of the dimensions of the changed meanings of knowledge in the modern university as they are related to the cultural and political crisis of our time. It even ventures a few proposals for reconstruction.

FEBRUARY 9, 1967

During the recent crisis on the Berkeley campus, the favorite quotation among the *cognoscenti* was Marx's aphorism that great historical events occur twice, "the first time as tragedy, the second as farce." Two years ago, the Berkeley campus was shaken by a series of events culminating on December 2, 1964, with a mass sit-in by the students, followed by mass arrests. What might have been a tragedy was averted by the faculty resolutions of

December 8, 1964, which recognized the fundamental political principles for which the students had contended. The faculty declared that there should be no University regulation of the content of speech or advocacy, and only such regulation of the time, place, and manner of political activity as was needed to prevent interference with normal University functions. The crisis had been over political rights and the faculty had responded with a constitutional solution.

When the old administration was replaced, first by the interim regime of Martin Meyerson and then, in the summer of 1965, by the new administration of Roger Heyns, all of the auguries were favorable. In outlook the new chancellor was liberal, and in action he was committed to the principle of consultation. He appointed to his staff several professors who were prominent in the struggle for the resolutions of December 8. Unlike previous chancellors, he was not harassed by outside meddling, either from the state-wide university administration or from the Regents. During the past year, for example, President Kerr kept a prudent distance from Berkeley controversies.

November 30, 1966, Berkeley students again sat in; police were again called to the campus, and on December 2 the students voted to strike against the University. Had 1964 really been farce and was 1966 to end as tragedy? Although there are coincidences in chronology between the events of 1964 and those of 1966, the setting differed in important ways. The crisis of 1964 extended over several months, thus allowing the contestants time to formulate fairly coherent positions. The crisis of 1966 erupted suddenly, catching all parties off guard. This was most evident in the case of the faculty which, unprepared and without a position, was reduced to a promiscuous search for consensus. In 1964 the politics of the Free Speech Movement had a kind of radical purity: the students focused on political objectives and pursued them with an idealism similar to that of the heroic phase of the civil rights movement. In 1966 student political orientations had been shaped by the growth of "New Left" doctrines, by participation in the Congressional campaign of Robert Scheer, by continuous protests against the Vietnam war, and by endless disputes with the Administration concerning political rights and due process on campus. Thus, in 1964 the students claimed "constitutional rights"; in 1966 they demanded "student power." Also, between 1964 and 1966 the graduate teaching assistants organized into a trade union and many of them took a certain pride in their worker status. "The issue here," explained the student president of the union during the crisis, "is working conditions. As long as the police are used in this way, we can't work." Along with the unionists another and more exotic element entered the movement: the cool and hippie culture of Telegraph Avenue with its distinctive blend of student and non-student styles. In 1964 the politicos had been impatient with and distrustful of the hippies; at the very end of the 1966 crisis Mario Savio, who had been the student leader of FSM in 1964 but was now a non-student leader of the new alliance, gave a benediction calling for a "coalition between student politios and hippies." Thus by 1966 a new culture had come into being, one which escapes the categories of the settlement of 1964.

Of all the differences, the most striking was the difference in mood. In 1964 the campus had a wealth of idealism and hope; the FSM had been good-natured, ironical, and humorous. In the months before the present crisis, the campus was tired, humorless, and disillusioned. During and after the crisis it was, above all, fearful. Not only had internal battles taken their toll, but the outside world had become more menacing. Governor Reagan had made the Berkeley campus a major campaign issue and had promised to establish an investigating commission headed by John McCone, former director of the CIA.

If there is a tragedy in the making, it will not be merely the result of what state politicians may do in the future, but of what the University has failed to do in the recent past. During the past two years, the campus has grown more and more distracted by political controversy. But the underlying causes are not being searched out. Until they are, political questions will continue to bedevil the campus, for all the worry and despair which arise from a fundamentally deranged community are being poured into the political arena. The behavior of faculty, students, and administrators reminds one of Santayana's fanatic, who redoubles his energy as he loses sight of his goal.

This is not to say that there are no genuine questions concerning political activity on campus. It is only to say that those questions have assumed disproportionate significance. Nor is it to say that the principles of 1964 were incorrect or unimportant. They spoke to real needs, and subsequent events have shown that too many people, on and off the campus, never understood or accepted them. It is only to say that 1964 brought not a hopeful peace but an uneasy truce; not a solution of the basic moral and intellectual questions, but only an opportunity, thus far unused, and now rapidly disappearing, for facing those questions.

Over the past two years the truce was often strained, and on several occasions nearly broke down. Increasing numbers of students began to doubt the Administration's loyalty to the principles of political freedom. Students felt that they were not given a fair voice in the formulation of the rules governing political activity. A year-long effort to revise the constitution of student government, so as to give it more autonomy, came to nothing when the new constitution was brusquely termed "illegal" by Administration spokesmen. At the request of the House Committee on Un-American Activities, the University handed over the names of student political leaders without their knowledge and consent, and when an Oakland taxpayer sued the University to make those names available to any citizen, the University's lawyer sided with the taxpayer in court. The Chancellor frequently expressed his disgust with the quality of the political meetings held in Sproul Plaza (symbolic home of 1964's Free Speech Movement) and talked about removing the rallies to some less conspicuous corner of the campus. The Vietnam Day Committee and the Administration were constantly at loggerheads, and many students came to feel that the Administration hated the VDC's doctrine and style more than it loved the principles of political freedom. A student who excoriated one of the deans in a letter to the student newspaper was threatened with punishment. These and similar events brought the students to the point where they had little trust in the bureaucracy.

The resolutions of 1964 spawned a generation of pettifoggers who argued furiously over such matters as the precise size and location of tables, the distribution of literature, the regulation of parades, and the size of posters. As the issues grew more legalistic, the passions aroused grew more intense and the disputants less capable of self-examination. For one antic moment in 1965, Berkeley was without a chancellor and the state-wide university without a president. Both resigned when a puckish demonstrator hoisted a banner bearing the terrible four-letter word. The demonstrator maintained that the Word stood for Freedom Under Clark Kerr, but everyone else insisted that the struggle was over rules and that there was nothing funny about it.

Gradually a certain mood and a certain political style began to dominate campus life. The mood was one of hostility and despair; the style one of confrontation. The two sides met as adversaries in a hopeless game, and, to a remarkable degree, both accepted the same definition of the rules of the game. Both sides agreed that the over-all character of the contest was political, that the action took the form of a battle, with a winner and a loser, and that confrontation was the appropriate style of behavior.

Thus, the students theorized that they were confronting a "power structure" bound by strong and subtle links to the larger power structures of state and nation. The objectives of the national power elite were empire abroad and the suppression of dissent at home. The University Administration's target was "the student movement," which stood for peace, civil rights, and radical social change. Hence, if the Administration won, the children of light lost. During the struggle every Administration move had to be probed for its "real" meanings. This view, obviously, made no allowance for mistakes, accidents, or common stupidity, let alone for good will.

The Administration had its own version of the power elite theory: in its view the University's troubles were the work of a hard core of non-student agitators, plus a small number of student activists, who persistently abused the generous freedoms allowed on campus. Their goal was either to wreck the University or take it over. The "silent majority" of unpolitical students and a few hundred unrealistic faculty members had been duped by the agitators, thereby aggravating the Administration's task.

Starting from these shared premises, relations between the combatants followed ritual patterns and ritual forensics. Each side was helplessly dependent on the other. Each could predict the other's tactics. Trapped by theory, neither had the freedom to deal radically with the fundamental malaise of which the endless controversies over rules were only symptoms.

Thus, when the Administration proposed moving the Free Forum, with its mass rallies and raucous microphone, from Sproul Plaza to a less visible part of the campus, the students "knew" that this was another move to escalate the campaign against student dissent. The Chancellor predictably replied that the Forum in Sproul Plaza fostered

> . . . a style of speech that is often vicious in intent, dishonest, laced with slander and character assassination, indifferent to evidence and truth, contemptuous of disagreement, and often charged with hatred.

The microphone was "primarily an organizational weapon. . . . Its frequent use is coercive and its main target is the University itself." The students responded that the Administration's standard of style was all too clear: just as the administrators admired a desk free of clutter, so too they desired a campus free of dissident students.

The Administration asserted that the mass rallies and agitation were making the campus "unstable," even "ungovernable." While retreating from its intention of moving the microphone, the Administration warned that "the days of doing business on this campus by coercion . . . are over." The students agreed that the question was one of power, and that the microphone and the Forum were their essential weapons. They countered the Administration's conception of power as the ability to enforce rules by demanding greater student participation in rule-making and adjudication. Inevitably, they raised the banner of "Student Power"–inevitable because authority had disappeared and only power mattered. Each side saw any action of the other as an "escalation" of the conflict, to which a "response" must be made.

The sterility of the shared premises became manifest in the self-contradictory aims announced by each side. Ever since 1964, the students had castigated the University for its bureaucratism, its maze of rules, and its intricate procedures. Now they were demanding additional rules, new procedures, and more machinery. Having first attacked the machine, the students next complicated its structure, and were now demanding a greater part in running it. No Administration theorist was able to see that here, proposed by the students themselves, was a "final solution" to the student question: administrators and students, working together, might construct a machine capable of swallowing 27,500 students forever.

The Administration caught itself in a different trap. A huge and complex campus necessarily looks to the administration as the continuing center of energy and direction, especially when that campus must face profound tasks of reform within and hostility without. The faculty is incapable of sustained action. But instead of directing the energy and idealism generated by 1964 toward reconstruction, the Administration at Berkeley insisted that the primary problem was order. While faculty members and students pleaded for new directions, the Administration replied that it was so absorbed with the "fallout" from the Plaza that reform had to await the solution of the political problem. It seems never to have occurred to the Chancellor and his many assistants that they had formulated the problem in such a way that it could not be solved. Order, as they defined it, was unattainable. Short of a repudiation of the December 8 resolutions, which would have brought instant chaos, there was no conceivable way of exorcising the student activists, of preventing students and non-students from mingling, or of lessening the deep revulsion against the corruptness of American society and the horrors of Vietnam. The Administration's deepest intellectual and moral failure was its failure to understand that it was directing an educational community. Its deepest psychological and political failure was lack of political foresight: it was willing to use force—even outside police force—to secure order, but it was silent as to how it would then gain the future trust, cooperation, and enthusiasm of those whom it had determined to pacify.

There was, then, a fatal logic in this politics of confrontation, in this academic re-enactment of game theory. Once the premises were set, a showdown was inevitable; the more rationally each side acted out the shared premises, the more profoundly irrational would the final outcome be. All that was needed was a triggering event.

For some years the Navy has been coming to campus to recruit future sailors. In early 1965, when the Navy set up a recruiting table, students picketed it. They also submitted a formal complaint to the Administration, asking why governmental agencies should enjoy privileges on campus not accorded to other non-student organizations. The Administration took no action.

On November 28, 1966, the Navy again set up a recruiting table in the lobby of the Student Union Building. The Executive Vice Chancellor claims that elected student officers consented to the placing of the table, but the chief student officers have flatly contradicted this assertion, saying that in fact they had advised against it.

For two days the Navy quietly performed its duty, but the Students for a Democratic Society (SDS) were working too. They were planning an action which would simultaneously oppose the war in Vietnam and show the inequity in the Administration's application of the rules governing the use of campus facilities by off-campus organizations. Their method was to set up a table for the dissemination of material opposed to the war and the draft. This table would be placed beside the Navy table, and it would be manned by a non-student. At the same time, students would form a picket around the Navy table.

On Wednesday morning, November 30, the non-student (a lady member of an anti-draft organization) asked the Dean of Students for permission to set up her table. Her request was refused. Nonetheless, she returned to the Student Union Building and set up a table alongside the Navy's with a sign offering "Alternatives to Military Service." Shortly after noon the SDS pickets arrived and formed their line.

Soon after the pickets came the police, and also the reporters and cameramen. The scene quickly attracted a fair-sized crowd, some sympathetic to the demonstration, some opposed, and some just curious.

At this point, a campus policeman told the anti-draft lady that she would have to leave. After a brief argument she agreed, and the police started to carry her table through the crowd. Many bystanders loudly protested the removal of the table, and several tried to grab it, making the police jerk it from their hands. Just then, a former football player shoved through the crowd, apparently in an attempt to clear a path for the police. Several students shouted at the football player to stop pushing people around. The football player turned, and, according to several witnesses, struck a student in the mouth. When the person who was struck lunged at his attacker he was restrained and led away by policemen. The crowd grew resentful and apprehensive. In order to reduce confusion and the possibility of more violence and arrests, several students urged the crowd to sit down. Within moments, some seventy-five or one hundred people sat down around the Navy table, jamming the lobby of the Student Union. They began discussions about the arrest and about the Navy's special privileges.

Around 1 P.M. some notables began to arrive, including the president of the student body, the Vice Chancellor for Student Affairs, and Mario Savio, Berkeley's most famous non-student. (Savio was denied readmission to Berkeley for passing out leaflets on campus while not a student.)

The Vice Chancellor told the demonstrators that he was willing to talk with the students, but not under coercion, and that unless the crowd dispersed he would declare the assembly unlawful. Campus policemen closed all entrances to the lower lobby of the Student Union

Building, permitting people to leave but not to enter. Three officers also barricaded the stairway leading to the main floor, preventing the persons in the main lobby from joining those in the lower lobby. The three officers were slowly being pushed down the stairs when the barricade broke and students poured into the lower lobby.

Order was soon restored, and the discussions continued. The demonstrators agreed to disperse if the anti-draft table were permitted to remain, if no charges were pressed against the student who had been led away by the police, and if no disciplinary actions were taken against the demonstrators. The Vice Chancellor agreed to let the table remain if a student manned it, but he said that he could not promise amnesty for the demonstrators, and that the case of the arrested student was out of his hands. Further discussion produced no agreement. The Vice Chancellor declared the assembly unlawful and left. The demonstrators stayed.

While all this was going on downstairs, a crowd of several thousand had formed outside the building and in its main lobby. A degree of organization and leadership emerged among the demonstrators. The talk turned to "student power," the sins of administration, and the failures of the faculty. "Happy Birthday" was sung for Mario's year-old son, and when the Navy left at about 4 P.M., the demonstrators gave them a hearty "Anchors Aweigh."

Shortly after 6 P.M., some twenty or thirty off-campus police entered the locked building. The demonstrators inside had no way of knowing the policemen's intention: did they intend to arrest only a few, or were they going to carry everyone away, in a re-enactment of 1964? The police, holding warrants signed by the Executive Vice Chancellor, arrested six persons, all non-students, on charges of trespassing and creating a public nuisance. Chaos threatened when the police attempted to drag the first person from the crowd of seated protestors. Some persons shrieked in alarm. Others shouted abusively at the officers, and pulled at their arms and legs, getting hit and kicked in return. The other arrests were accomplished without incident. None of the six resisted. Among those arrested were Savio and Jerry Rubin, local leader of the VDC.

Administration spokesmen have offered a very different account of these events. The Executive Vice Chancellor was reported in the student newspaper as saying that the six were arrested because they played "the key role" in the sit-in. In an official statement to the faculty and staff, he said that "the demonstration today was initiated and led by non-students in direct defiance of University regulations." On the other hand, three faculty eyewitnesses, in a signed document, have reported that "none of the six seemed involved as initiators," that one of the six did not speak throughout the demonstration, and that "two others participated minimally if at all." When confronted with these statements, one of the Chancellor's assistants said that the Administration had put up with "eighteen months of activists' blackmail" before moving against the non-students. The Chancellor himself, addressing the Academic Senate, stated that the whole thing began when "non-students attempted in violation of our rules to set up a table. . . ." He referred to other recent "provocations," and concluded that "we are dealing, then, not with a single incident but with a chronic condition."

These Administration statements overlooked certain

critical distinctions among the groups of people involved in the early stages of the disturbance: (1) the non-student who set up the antiwar table but was not arrested; (2) the students who, after seeing one of their number struck, sat in; and (3) the six arrested non-students, who by no account initiated or organized the demonstration. It appears that the Administration, acting on its "outside agitator" theory, was out to get these people, even if that meant calling police onto the campus and committing a public injustice against individuals.

As the police van moved away, another violent encounter took place. Hundreds of students jammed the street around the van. They were swept aside by a phalanx of policemen. Many persons were shoved and clubbed, some severely. Three students were arrested for interfering with the police.

The Student Union Building was now unlocked, and the demonstrators outside were able to join those inside. They began a marathon mass meeting. By 10 P.M. the crowd had grown to around 3,000, jammed into a large ballroom. Many speakers stressed the futility of trying to negotiate reasonably with the Administration over questions of political activity. The Executive Vice Chancellor appeared for about a half hour to answer questions. The hostile audience clearly considered his statements to be evasive or even false, and he was loudly hooted. Savio, who had returned after posting bail, was the last speaker of the evening. He recounted the unsuccessful efforts of individuals to gain due process during the last two years, and described a student strike as the "least disruptive way of pressuring the Administration." At 1 A.M. the students voted, nearly unanimously, to strike. The campus community was offered coffee and rebellion for breakfast.

The next day (December 2, two years to the day after the mass sit-in and arrests of 1964) a rally of about 8,000 confirmed the decision and accepted the demands of the strike: that police must never be called on campus to "solve" political problems; no disciplinary action against participants; off-campus individuals and noncommercial groups should have privileges on campus equal to those enjoyed by governmental agencies; disciplinary hearings must in the future be open and conducted according to the canons of due process; discussions must begin toward the creation of effective student representation on rule-making bodies. The Teaching Assistants' Union, the student government, and (later) the student newspaper all supported the strike. Chancellor Heyns, who had been away, returned to an embattled campus.

Throughout the rest of the week the strike and mass rallies continued. Groups of faculty met frequently to discuss the issues and prepare for the forthcoming meeting of the Academic Senate. The Chancellor declared himself opposed to the strike and refused to meet with representatives of the strikers.

The strike itself was well organized, but there are no reliable estimates concerning its effectiveness. Although there are a marvelous range and variety of political groups on the Berkeley campus, there was little factionalism or doctrinal infighting apparent in the conduct of the strike. For some time now most campus political groups have united in a loose confederal structure, called the Council of Campus Organizations, for the purpose of doing battle with the Administration over issues concerning the legitimacy of the rules governing political activity. Hence, the many organizations participating in the strike had a pre-established system of discussion and communication.

Perhaps the two most powerful new forces on the campus political scene are the Teaching Assistants' Union and the Free University of Berkeley. The former has a membership of about 400 graduate teaching assistants and is affiliated with the AFT. The union voted to strike, supported it to the end, and supplied many of its leaders. The Free University is a "counter-institution" offering courses in everything from psychedelics and modern painting to Marxism and the theory and practice of imperialism. Some 250 persons are in some sense enrolled in the Free University, and some of the strike's leaders are closely associated with it. The strikers quickly elected an executive committee and a negotiating committee, proving once again that Berkeley students have a trained capacity for political organization and action. They can produce a manifesto and arrange a demonstration at a moment's notice. Many of the students have become impressive political speakers and tacticians. While the campus Administration intones the language of community, it is the students who have been actually building community among themselves. Although there are student leaders, there is no permanent clique which can manipulate the students. The movement waxes and wanes, leaders come and go as the situation changes. When the right conditions appear, thousands of students with a shared orientation can be mobilized within hours. If the Administration tries to destroy this community by chopping off its head, it may find itself battling a Hydra.

The Senate meeting of December 5 opened with an address by the Chancellor. He reaffirmed his opposition to the strike, rejected amnesty for rule violators, called the rules "fair and equitable," argued that present hearing procedures met "the highest standards of judicial fairness," and asked for confidence from the faculty. The Senate debated and approved by a vote of 795 to 28, with 143 abstentions, a compromise, omnibus resolution. On the one hand, the Senate called for an end to the strike and affirmed "confidence in the Chancellor's leadership." On the other hand, it urged amnesty for students who had violated rules during the course of the strike. The Senate declared that tactics of "mass coercion" and the use of external police, except in extreme emergency, were both inappropriate to a university. The resolution also asked that new avenues be explored for increasing student participation in rule-making and enforcement, and called for a faculty-student commission "to consider new modes of governance and self-regulation in the University."

Unlike December, 1964, no one was enthusiastic about the result. Many faculty members wanted a more outspoken condemnation of the decision to bring the police on campus. A smaller number was disappointed that the Senate had not even discussed the matter of the arrest of the six non-students. A near majority, sick of the turmoil and persuaded that it had been caused by a few troublemakers, narrowly failed to pass a "hard" resolution supporting the Chancellor without reservation. No one spoke in defense of the students. Only a few dared to challenge the official theory that a small band of subversives had caused the trouble. None dared to say openly what many had declared privately, that the Administration's decision to call in the police was more than a mistake: it was a crime. The fragile compromise in the resolutions caused the faculty liberals to abstain from vigorous debate for fear that the resolutions would be mutilated by amendments. Consequently, the speeches were made by the faculty conservatives and many were harsh. One compared the Berkeley demonstrators to the Nazi students who had driven the non-Nazi professors from Germany. Another member finished his long speech by declaring in exasperation that he didn't want to hear any more arguments, only a vote of confidence in defense of order and authority. Thus the liberal faculty left the meeting frustrated by their silence and uncertain of their achievement; the conservatives left fulfilled by their rhetoric but somewhat resentful of the result.

It is doubtful that the Chancellor was pleased by resolutions which coupled police action with the student strike and condemned both; nor could the faculty declaration for amnesty be viewed by him as other than a rebuff. The students interpreted the resolution as final evidence of faculty unreliability.

> The faculty cannot solve our problems [declared a student manifesto]. They did not choose to implement the December 8 Resolution, and [they have] demonstrated their inability to deal . . . with the educational ills of the University.

Thus the faculty managed to disappoint itself, the Administration, and the students.

The next day the Board of Regents met in emergency session. Regent Edwin Pauley, who had declared that "if people on the payroll can't understand their conditions of employment they shouldn't be there, and I'm for getting rid of them," introduced a resolution calling for retroactive punishment of striking teaching assistants and faculty. It was defeated and a substitute was passed which supported the Chancellor, refrained from punishing the students, and condemned the "interference" of "outsiders." "The Regents support all necessary action to preserve order on all campuses of the University." Separating the student strikers from their supporters among the teaching assistants and faculty, the Regents produced the only unequivocal action of the week, a resolution which radically redefined the nature of academic freedom and tenure. Henceforth

> University personnel . . . who participate in any strike or otherwise fail to meet their assigned duties, in an effort to disrupt University administration, teaching, or research, will thereby be subject to termination of their employment . . . , denial of re-employment or the imposition of other appropriate sanctions.

Obviously, the Regents had sown the seeds of future controversy.

Meanwhile the politicians of the state were angrily demanding that the striking faculty and teaching assistants be dismissed. The Governor-elect warned the students to

> . . . obey the prescribed rules or get out. . . . The people of California . . . have a right to lay down rules and a code of conduct for those who accept that gift [of public education].

The president *pro tem* of the Senate advised Reagan that all that the University needed was "a new president and some regents with more guts than liberalism." The Speaker of the Assembly, and sometime Chubb Fellow of Yale, who had gotten his investigating committee from the 1964 crisis, made his usual statesmanlike suggestion: instead of appointing a new commission, the Governor should appoint the former CIA head to the Board of

Regents. As of this writing, a bill has been introduced into the state legislature which would drastically reduce the powers of the Regents and place the University under closer legislative control.

The strike dragged to a close that evening and a haggard faculty and student body prepared for finals. In their last mass meeting, the students found a measure of joy and humor—graces sadly lacking this time. Half the joy was relief: they had been naughty, but hadn't gotten spanked too hard, at least not yet. There also emerged at the rally a spontaneous coalition between the hippies and the political activists. While the teaching assistants, like good trade unionists, sang "Solidarity Forever" in one room, the hippie-activist coalition sang "Yellow Submarine" in another, and promised that next term they would "blow the Administration's mind." Instead of resorting to such "square" tactics as strikes and sit-ins, they might clog the machine, mock its logic, and drive its operators out of their minds by such tactics as flooding the deans with thousands of petitions, misplacing their identity cards, returning books to the wrong libraries, flocking to the student clinic for all manner of psychosomatic complaints, and wearing masks to class. It is impossible to anticipate how the Chancellor will respond to that escalation.

It is doubtful whether the strike settled anything. Surely it added to the legacy of bitterness and anxiety. Perhaps it provided the jolt needed to start the University on the work of self-examination which it has so far shirked. More likely, Berkeley will enter an era of strong solutions—an obsession with total control, possibly a purge of dissident elements. That way may bring peace, but it will be the peace of intellectual and moral torpor.

The only hope for the University lies in replacing the narrow and fatal premises which have produced the present impasse with others more appropriate to the general social situation in which the University now stands. That social situation is one that can be called revolutionary in the sense that while the forces of change gather momentum, the society cannot find the appropriate response either in thought or act.

The troubles which beset American society are unprecedented and paradoxical. Stated broadly, our condition is one of widespread affluence, rising social expectations, scientific and technological dynamism, extensive welfare programs, and a high degree of formal democracy. In spite of all this, there is pervasive contempt for the very system which has given its members more comfort and leisure than any society in history. There is in this progressive, tolerant, and literate society a frightening lack of intelligent loyalty and spontaneous affection for the system. Above all, there lurks the fear that behind the greatest concentration of economic, scientific, and military power in history there is a moral weakness so thoroughgoing that when the society faces a substantive problem, such as racial discrimination, its cities are thrown into turmoil, or when it becomes embroiled in a foreign policy misadventure, its political creativity is limited to throwing increasing military might against a small country in a cause whose hopelessness rises in direct ratio to the violence employed.

Historically, revolutions have been occasions for attempting something new in the political world: a new vision of society, a new concept of authority, a new ideal of freedom or justice. We are accustomed to think of revolutions as arising out of poverty and injustice, exacerbated by the governing class's refusal to "modernize"– France of 1789, Russia of 1917, China of 1945. But the revolution brewing in America, this richest and most advanced of societies, is different. It is nourished by a sense of failure rather than hope. Our physical success is accompanied by spiritual despair. America is proving that modern man can create dazzlingly powerful and rich societies in which the rate of change is so intense that men cannot endure it, let alone master it. The paradox of our revolutionary condition, then, is the existence of despair, disaffection, and contempt within a society that is prosperous, progressive, and democratic.

Berkeley is the perfect example of the kind of university which a democratic and progressive society might be expected to produce. Its faculty is distinguished, its students highly selected, and its facilities superb. Like the society around it, the University is dynamic and growing, and it can claim excellence in science and professional training. Despite these achievements, it is a university which its administrators find ungovernable, its educational leaders find unreformable, and its students find unlivable. For two years its life has been marked by an enervating anxiety and hostility which cannot be dismissed as a "failure in communication." The melancholy truth is that there is little to communicate because there is no widely shared understanding about the meaning and purpose of the institution. Lacking the unifying force which flows spontaneously from common understandings, the system is held together by a bureaucratic organization whose weakness is exposed whenever it is directly challenged.

This is partly the result of Berkeley's legacy as a public university, a legacy which contrasts with the traditional idea informing the ancient public universities of Europe, as well as the private universities and colleges of this country.

The striking difference between the traditional university and the modern public university is best seen in the small place assigned to administration in the former. The older university could flourish with a "housekeeper" administration because of one basic presupposition: that a genuine and autonomous community of scholars existed to be served. The modern public university, however, was born in a state of dependence on the outside society and, in most instances, the administration was created first. It never had the chance to become a community. Its survival depended upon public support and administrative power, not on the moral and intellectual fellowship of its members.

The public university adheres to a conception of knowledge which differs greatly from that of its ancestors. The knowledge it produces must be useful to the social and economic interests of an expanding society. At Berkeley, there are installations, institutes, and laboratories in which trained experts develop knowledge in such fields as naval medicine, sanitary engineering, space science, marine food resources, traffic engineering, forest products, nuclear weapons, mining, and range management. The demand for all these services is strong and growing. But it goes without saying that there is no irresistible demand that the university preserve the knowledge and experience of the past or encourage reflection on the intangibles of the good life. The old idea of the university as a community of conversants has been pushed aside by the Baconian vision of knowledge as power. But practicality has not by itself created the ideal of knowledge which now threatens all universities, public or private. The notorious concern of most faculties with publication and research is directly related to the requirement that a scholar be "original." He must turn up novelties of fact or theory, and his novelties must pay off, either because they are practical or because they "generate" further research. Knowledge is no longer associated with wisdom, or with the fruits of contemplation or rediscovery. It is not guided by reflection, but fired by the hope of a "breakthrough." This conception of knowledge brings a new pace to academic life: the researcher is forever racing to the frontiers where the future beckons. He must continuously invent new concepts, models, and techniques. The greatest sin lies not in being trivial, but in appearing old-fashioned.

At Berkeley these concerns amount to an obsession. It is virtually official doctrine that the ruthless pursuit of productivity is the key to Berkeley's rapid rise to a position where it is no longer just "another state university," but can compare with such renowned institutions as Harvard.

The assumption that a university is a place where knowledge is "pursued" and "cumulated" seems harmless enough until its effects are considered. This approach entails destruction of and contempt for the old, and for the fuddy-duddies who profess it. The perfect illustration of the new spirit is the popularity of Whitehead's battle cry among social scientists: "A science which hesitates to forget its founders is lost." Forgetting and destroying are necessary preconditions for productivity: he travels fastest who travels lightest; he travels lightest who sheds civility, tradition, and care for the common culture of the intellect.

The new conception of knowledge produces human casualties as well. In departments throughout Berkeley there are endless macabre discussions, amounting to ritual murder, about the older professors left stranded alongside the mainstream of research. Young men are ready, but the old men are protected by tenure. The curiosity is that the superannuated professor is probably in his thirties.

The competitive ethos of the modern research-oriented university has created "dysfunctional" or "deviant" human types, to use the current idiom. These are, lamentably, the very types which were "functional" in the traditional university. Foremost among them is the teacher. The teacher who is threatened is not the one who loves to be surrounded by admiring undergraduates and who makes a cult of non-writing, but rather the one who naïvely believes that teaching and research can be creatively combined. But, as an academic member of the Berkeley Administration responsible for promoting educational reform has said, "A professor's bread is buttered by his relationships within his field, and they are established by research. You don't get an international reputation for giving a great course at Berkeley." Nor need the academic face a Kierkegaardian choice between teaching and research. Numerous agencies are eager to pay for the professor's "released time" from the classroom so that he can pursue his research free from the distractions of teaching. In some fields it is tacitly agreed that the professors who carry normal teaching loads are those whose research is not so valuable as to justify their giving full time to it.

If the teacher is "dysfunctional," the student is worse. To the jet-age frontiersman he is a distraction and an anomaly, except when he is an apprentice researcher.

Most graduate students present few problems, for they have been "socialized" and can even instruct their seniors in the art of grantsmanship. Those undergraduates and graduates who are left outside the system and who feel hurt and betrayed have formulated their own counteridea of knowledge. Against the professionalism of the insiders, they proclaim the primacy of passion, subjectivity, and openness. Knowledge which is not obviously related to their immediate personal needs and situation is irrelevant. To be relevant, knowledge must speak *now* to *their* needs. The ancient values of detachment and disinterested inquiry are seen as evasions of responsibility; or, worse, as typifying the vice of "objectivism" which transforms thought and feeling into alienated objects and serves as an ideological fig leaf for a corrupt establishment.

It would be a foolish man who, given the complex problems confronting the modern university, would claim to have a new constitution in his pocket. Nevertheless, certain things are clear. If something of the traditional idea of the university is to be salvaged, there must be a revitalization of a common culture and a lessening of the centrifugal tendencies of specialization. It must be recognized that the pursuit of knowledge can take forms incompatible with the unique cultural and educational character of the university. This is not to say that the university should turn away from new modes of knowledge and inquiry and lovingly cultivate all that is precious and old. A creative tension between tradition and innovation should be the guiding principle.

It has become clear that the University of California is no longer viable in its present form. The whole vast state-wide complex, with its centralized bureaucratic apparatus of control, should be decentralized toward something like a "Commonwealth of Campuses" model, but it is unlikely that this will happen. Two years ago, a committee appointed by the Regents proposed that the state-wide system be devolved into a looser alliance of largely autonomous campuses. After creating a brief sensation, the report was conveniently forgotten. The best hope for the future lies in devising ways to reintegrate faculty and students around smaller structures which are allowed genuine powers of decision-making and broad opportunities for educational experiments. If smaller communities are to be established, there must be serious open-minded discussion of the possibilities of student participation in a far broader range of University matters than hitherto.

At this moment, the Academic Senate is considering a concrete proposal to establish a student-faculty commission to explore ways of improving "the participation of students in the formulation of educational policies, including measures for the improvement of teaching." The proposal lays special emphasis on the need to develop "patterns of student-faculty cooperation" at the departmental level.

These proposals move in the direction recently suggested by President Kerr. In a newspaper interview of a month ago, he described Berkeley's steps toward educational reform as "somewhat too conservative." He also said that

> . . . the University of California had the most restrictive policies [regarding] political activity of any university I've ever known about, outside a dictatorship.

He also declared "that this is a generation that wants to

participate" and "there ought to be 100, or 1,000 opportunities" for it to do so.

In contrast, too many faculty members have resisted trying to understand the contemporary student and have indulged themselves, instead, in grotesque analogies between Berkeley and Latin American-style universities or Nazi youth movements. The spectral analogies, like the outside agitator theory, are appeals to fear and rest upon the belief that men can be frightened into order.

Today's student finds himself in a world of complexity and change, of exciting possibilities and ominous threats, of uncertain landmarks for personal conduct and all too certain prescriptions for success in the straight world. He sees a world whose promise is constantly violated by destruction, discrimination, and cruelty. In an older and simpler age he would have entered the university with greater confidence and stability, for many institutions would have helped to prepare him for adulthood. But family, church, neighborhood, and school have now declined in effectiveness, and where they once contributed to his confidence, they now reinforce his uncertainty. Consequently, the student is led to demand more from his university experience than ever before. Such students embarrass the university for the same reason that Kierkegaard embarrassed Christendom: by the purity of their demands. They want the university to be a place where education and knowledge are pursued out of love for the pursuit itself. They are in revolt against all that is remote and impersonal in human relations. They want an educational community whose members will look at each other, not one in which relationships are defined by rules and treated as simple problems of order and compliance. Because they take the democratic ideal seriously, they want a voice in the decisions which shape their lives. It is these students who provide hope.

Opportunities for creative change still exist at Berkeley, but the problems are profound, reflecting as they do the sickness of our society and the disaffection of a whole generation. This time the campus must face the future with a fuller appreciation of the radical nature of the reforms needed.

III
The Battle of People's Park

The events related here constitute the first application of systematic terror directed at an American campus by its own authorities. Within one year after People's Park such scenes had become familiar: Jackson State, Kent State, and the Isla Vista student community of Santa Barbara, among others, also experienced the new methods of campus pacification. But People's Park was first, and both participants and observers were shocked by the scale of official violence.

*It should be mentioned that the allegations of brutality made by many of the persons who were swept in by the mass arrest and sent to Santa Rita Prison have now been largely confirmed by a grand jury investigation. (*Alameda County Grand Jury Report on People's Park Disorders and the Santa Rita Jail, *November 1, 1969.) Indictments against those arrested have been dropped and some prison officers have been punished. As of this writing, the disputed piece of land remains an all but deserted parking lot. A private company contracted with the University to run it under very generous terms, but soon gave up for want of customers.*

This essay also explores the logic of bureaucracy when confronted by genuine human novelty, and argues that the violence that destroyed People's Park was the logical outcome of certain conceptions of knowledge, rationality, and order.

JUNE 19, 1969

Shortly before 5:00 A.M., on Thursday, May 15, 1969, a motley group of about fifty hippies and "street-people" were huddled together on a lot 270 x 450 feet in Berkeley. The lot was owned by the Regents of the University of California and located a few blocks south of the Berkeley campus. Since mid-April this lot had been taken over and transformed into a "People's Park" by scores of people, most of whom had no connection with the University. Now the University was determined to reassert its legal rights of ownership. A police officer approached the group and announced that it must leave or face charges of trespassing. Except for three persons, the group left and the area was immediately occupied and surrounded by about 200 police from Berkeley, Alameda County, and the campus. The police were equipped with flak jackets, tear gas launchers, shotguns, and telescopic rifles. At 6:00 A.M. a construction crew arrived and by mid-afternoon an eight-foot steel fence encircled the lot.

At noon a rally was convened on campus and about 3,000 people gathered. The president-elect of the student body spoke. He started to suggest various courses of action that might be considered. The crowd responded to the first of these by spontaneously marching toward the lot guarded by the police. (For this speech, the speaker was charged a few days later with violating numerous campus rules, and, on the initiative of University officials, indicted for incitement to riot.) The crowd was blocked by a drawn police line. Rocks and bottles were thrown at the police, and the police loosed a tear gas barrage, scattering the crowd. Elsewhere, a car belonging to the city was burned. Meanwhile, police reinforcements poured in, soon reaching around 600. A rock was thrown from a roof-top and, without warning, police fired into a group on the roof of an adjacent building. Two persons were struck in the face by the police fire, another was blinded, probably permanently, and a fourth, twenty-five-year-old James Rector, later died. Before the day was over, at least thirty others were wounded by police gunfire and many more by clubs. One policeman received a minor stab wound and six more were reported as having been treated for minor cuts and bruises.

Meanwhile, action shifted to the campus itself, where police had herded a large crowd into Sproul Plaza by shooting tear gas along the bordering streets. The police then formed small detachments which continuously swept across the campus, breaking up groups of all sizes. Tear gas enfolded the main part of the campus and drifted into many of its buildings, as well as into the surrounding city. Nearby streets were littered with broken glass and rubble. At least six buckshot slugs entered the main library and three .38 caliber bullets lodged in the wall of a reference room in the same building. Before the day ended, more than ninety people had been injured by police guns and clubs.

Under a "State of Extreme Emergency" proclamation issued by Governor Reagan on February 5 in connection with the "Third World Strike" at Berkeley late last winter and never rescinded, a curfew was imposed on the city. Strict security measures were enforced on campus and in the nearby business districts, and all assemblies and rallies were prohibited. The proclamation also centralized control of the police under the command of Sheriff Frank Madigan of Alameda County.

Roger Heyns, the Chancellor of the University, saw none of this, for he had left the previous day for a meeting in Washington. His principal Vice Chancellor had gone to the Regents' meeting in Los Angeles. The Regents took notice of the events by declaring, "It is of paramount importance that law and order be upheld." The Governor said that the lot had been seized by the street-people "as an excuse for a riot." A Berkeley councilman called the previous use of the lot a "Hippie Disneyland freak show."

The next day, May 16, 2,000 National Guardsmen appeared in full battle dress, armed with rifles, bayonets, and tear gas. They were called into action by the Governor, but apparently the initiative came from local authorities acting in consultation with University administrators. Helicopters weaved back and forth over the campus and city. Berkeley was occupied. (The next day one helicopter landed on campus and an officer came out to ask that students stop flying their kites because the strings might foul his rotors. A collection was promptly taken and the sky was soon full of brightly colored kites.)

During the next few days a pattern emerged. Each day began quietly, almost like any other day, except that people awoke to the roar of helicopters and the rumble of transports. As University classes began (they had never been officially cancelled), the Guardsmen formed a line along the south boundary of the campus. The Guard and the police would cordon off the main plaza and station smaller detachments at various points around the campus.

Gradually the students crowded together, staring curiously at the Guardsmen and occasionally taunting them. The Guard stood ready with bayonets pointed directly at the crowd. This stand-off would continue for an hour or two, and then the police would charge the crowd with clubs and tear gas. The crowd would scatter, the police would give chase, the students and street-people would curse and sometimes hurl rocks or return tear gas canisters, and the police would beat or arrest some of them.

On Tuesday, May 20, the pattern and tempo changed. Previously the police had sought to break up gatherings on the campus, so now the protesters left the campus and began a peaceful march through the city. This was promptly stopped by the police. The marchers then filtered back to campus and a crowd of about 3,000 assembled. The group was pressed toward the Plaza by the police and Guardsmen and, when solidly hemmed in, was attacked by tear gas. A little later a helicopter flew low over the center of the campus and spewed gas over a wide area, even though the crowd had been thoroughly scattered. Panic broke out and people fled, weeping, choking, vomiting. Gas penetrated the University hospital, imperiling patients and interrupting hospital routines. It caused another panic at the University recreation area, nearly a mile from the center of campus, where many people, including mothers and children, were swimming. The police also threw gas into a student snack bar and into an office and classroom building.

The next day, May 21, was a turning point. More than 200 faculty members announced their refusal to teach; a local labor council condemned the police action; some church groups protested; and the newspapers and television stations began to express some criticism. Controversy arose over the ammunition which the police had used the previous Thursday. Sheriff Madigan was evasive about the size of birdshot issued, but the evidence was clear that buckshot had killed James Rector. The tear gas was first identified as the normal variety (CN) for crowd disturbances, but later it was officially acknowledged that a more dangerous gas (CS) was also used. The American army uses CS gas to flush out guerrillas in Vietnam. It can cause projectile vomiting, instant diarrhea and skin blisters, and even death, as it has to the VC, when the victim is tubercular. The Geneva Conventions outlaw the use of CS in warfare.

On the same day the Chancellor issued his first statement. He deplored the death which had occurred, as well as "the senseless violence." He warned that attempts were being made "to polarize the community and prevent rational solutions," and he stated that a university has a responsibility to follow "civilized procedures." Heyns made no criticism of the police or National Guard tactics: that same day a Guardsman had thrown down his helmet, dropped his rifle, and reportedly shouted, "I can't stand this any more." He was handcuffed, taken away for a physical examination, and then rushed off to a psychiatric examination. He was diagnosed as suffering from "suppressed aggressions."

In Sacramento, where a deputation of Berkeley faculty members was meeting with the Governor, aggression was more open. The Governor conceded that the helicopter attack might have been a "tactical mistake," but he also insisted that "once the dogs of war are unleashed, you must expect things will happen. . . ." Meantime, the statewide commander of the Guards defended the gas attack on the grounds that his troops were threatened. He noted that the general who ordered the attack had said, "It was a godsend that it was done at that time." The commander regretted the "discomfort and inconvenience to innocent bystanders," but added: "It is an inescapable by-product of combatting terrorists, anarchists, and hard-core militants on the streets and on the campus."

The next day, May 22, a peaceful march and flower-planting procession began in downtown Berkeley. With little warning, police and Guardsmen converged on the unsuspecting participants and swept them, along with a number of shoppers, newsmen, people at lunch, and a mailman, into a parking lot, where 482 were arrested, bringing the week's total near 800. As those arrested were released on bail, disturbing stories began to circulate concerning the special treatment accorded to "Berkeley types" in Santa Rita prison.

These stories, supported by numerous affidavits and news accounts submitted by journalists who had been bagged in the mass arrest, told of beatings, verbal abuse and humiliation, physical deprivations, and refusal of permission to contact counsel. Male prisoners told of being marched into the prison yard and forced to lie face down, absolutely motionless, on gravel and concrete for several hours. The slightest shift in posture, except for a head movement permitted once every half-hour, was met with a blow to the kidneys or testicles. On May 24 a district court judge issued an order restraining Sheriff Madigan's subordinates from beating and otherwise mistreating the arrestees taken to Santa Rita prison.

Despite all the arrests, the shotguns, gas, and clubs, the protesters have thus far shown remarkable restraint. Although both police and Guards have been targets of much foul language and some hard objects, nothing remotely resembling sustained violence has been employed against the police; and the Guard has been spared from all except verbal abuse. At this writing, the only damage to campus property, other than that caused by the police, has been two broken windows and one flooded floor.

After the mass arrests, the Governor lifted the curfew and the ban on assemblies, saying "a more controlled situation" existed. But he warned that no solution was likely until the troublemaking faculty and students were separated from the University. "A professional revolutionary group," he said, was behind it all. Charles Hitch, the President of the University of California, issued his first statement. (Much earlier, his own staff issued a statement protesting campus conditions of "intolerable stress" and physical danger.) The President ventured to criticize "certain tactics" of the police, but noted that these "were not the responsibility of university authorities."

In a television interview, the Chancellor agreed with the President, but added that negotiations were still possible because "we haven't stopped the rational process." A published interview (May 22) with the principal Vice Chancellor found him saying, "Our strategy was to act with humor and sensitivity. For instance, we offered to roll up the sod in the park and return it to the people. . . . We had no reason to believe there would be trouble." Meanwhile the Governor was saying, "The police didn't kill the young man. He was killed by the first college administrator who said some time ago it was all right to break laws in the name of dissent."

The Governor also accused the President of the University, a former Assistant Secretary of Defense and RANDsman, of "trying to weasel" to the side of the street-people. Two days later the Governor refused the request of the

Berkeley City Council to end the state of emergency and recall the Guard—requests, it might be added, that the University itself had not yet made. At this time the Mayor of Berkeley suggested that police tactics had been "clumsy and not efficient," to which Sheriff Madigan retorted: "If the Mayor was capable of running the city so well without problems we wouldn't be here. I advise the Mayor to take his umbrella and go to Berkeley's Munich. . . ."

On Friday, May 23, the Faculty Senate met. It listened first to a speech by the Chancellor in which he defined the occupation of the lot as an act of "unjustified aggression" against the University, and declared that the "avoidance of confrontations cannot be the absolute value." He said that the fence would remain as long as the issue was one of possession and control, and, pleading for more "elbow room," he asserted that the faculty should support or at least not oppose an Administrative decision once it had been made. The faculty then defeated a motion calling for the Chancellor's removal (94 voted for, 737 against, and 99 abstained). It approved, by a vote of 737 to 94, a series of resolutions which condemned what was called "as irresponsible a police and military reaction to a civic disturbance as this country has seen in recent times."

The resolutions demanded withdrawal of "the massive police and military presence on campus"; the "cessation of all acts of belligerency and provocation by demonstrators"; an investigation by the Attorney General of California and the Department of Justice; and the prompt implementation of a plan whereby part of the lot would become "an experimental community-generated park" and the fence would be simultaneously removed. The faculty also resolved to reconvene in a few days to reassess the situation.

There is where events now stand (May 26). But pressures

from all sides are increasing. A student referendum, which saw the heaviest turnout in the history of student voting, found 85 percent of the nearly 15,000 who voted favoring the use of the lot as it had been before the occupation. The students also voted to assess themselves $1.50 each quarter to help finance an ethnic studies department previously accepted by the University but now foundering. As of this writing, college students from all over the state are planning direct protests to Governor Reagan. Leaders of the protesters are preparing for a huge march against the fence on Memorial Day. The Governor remains committed to a hard line. All the issues remain unsettled.

What brought on this crisis? Like many of its sister institutions, the Berkeley campus has been steadily advancing its boundaries into the city. Back in 1956 it had announced its intention to purchase property in the area which includes the present disputed lot. Owing to its lack of funds, very little land was actually purchased. Finally, in June, 1967, the monies were allocated and the University announced that ultimately dormitories would be built on the land, but that in the interim it would be used for recreation.

The lot itself was purchased in 1968, but no funds were then available for development. Undoubtedly the University was aware of the disastrous experience of other academic institutions which had attempted to "redevelop" surrounding areas. In fact, a short time ago the University announced, with much fanfare, its intention to mount a major attack on the problems of the cities. Despite these professions, the University's treatment of its own urban neighbors has consisted of a mixture of middle-class prejudice, aesthetic blindness, and bureaucratic callousness.

The victims in this case, however, have not been so much the blacks as another pariah group, one whose identity is profoundly influenced by the University itself. For many years, Telegraph Avenue and "the south campus area" have constituted a major irritant to the University, the city fathers, and the business interests. It is the Berkeley demimonde, the place where students, hippies, dropouts, radicals, and runaways congregate. To the respectables, it is a haven for drug addicts, sex fiends, criminals, and revolutionaries. Until the University began its expansion, it was also an architectural preserve for fine old brown shingle houses and interesting shops. It is no secret that the University has long considered the acquisition of land as a means of ridding the area not of substandard housing, but of its human "blight." The disputed lot was the perfect symbol of the University's way of carrying out urban regeneration: first, raze the buildings; next let the land lie idle and uncared for; then permit it to be used as an unimproved parking lot, muddy and pitted; and finally, when the local people threaten to use and enjoy the land, throw a fence around it.

Around mid-April, a movement was begun by street-people, hippies, students, radicals, and a fair sprinkling of elderly free spirits to take over the parking lot and transform it. Many possibilities were discussed: a child care clinic; a crafts fair; a baseball diamond. Soon grass and shrubs were planted, playground equipment installed, benches built, and places made for eating, lounging, and occasional speechmaking. About 200 people were involved in the beginning, but soon the Park was intensively and lovingly used by children, the young, students and street-people, and the elderly. A week after the Park began, the University announced its intention to develop a playing field by July 1, and the Park people responded by saying that the University would have to fight for it. Discussions followed, but not much else. The University said, however, that no construction would be started without proper warning and that it was willing to discuss the future design of the field.

On May 8 the Chancellor agreed to form a committee representing those who were using the lot as well as the University. But he insisted as "an essential condition" of discussions about the future of the land that all work on the People's Park cease. In addition he announced certain guidelines for his committee: University control and eventual use must be assured; the field must not produce "police and other control problems"; and no political or public meetings were to be held on the land. Suddenly, on May 13, he announced his decision to fence in the area as the first step toward developing the land for intramural recreation. "That's a hard way to make a point," he said, "but that's the way it has to be. . . . The fence will also give us time to plan and consult. Regretfully, this is the only way the entire site can be surveyed, soil tested, and planned for development . . . hence the fence."

Why did it have to be this way? Because, as the Chancellor explained, it was necessary to assert the University's title to ownership. Concerning the apparent lack of consultation with his own committee, he said that a plan could not be worked out because the Park people had not only refused to stop cultivating and improving the land, but they had "refused to organize a responsible committee" for consultative purposes. In addition, he cited problems of health, safety, and legal liability, as well as complaints from local residents.

The first response came from the faculty chairman of the Chancellor's committee. He declared that the Chancellor had allowed only two days (the weekend) for the committee to produce a plan and that the "University didn't seem interested in negotiations." On May 14 a protest rally was held and the anarchs of the Park, surprisingly, pulled themselves together and formed a negotiating committee. Although rumors of an impending fence were circulating, spokesmen for the Park people insisted that they wanted discussion, not confrontation.

On May 15, the day immediately preceding the early morning police action, the Chancellor placed an advertisement in the campus newspaper inviting students to draw up "ideas or designs" for the lot and to submit them by May 21. The ad was continued even after the military occupation. On May 18, three days after the occupation had begun, the Chancellor announced that there would be "no negotiations in regard to the land known as People's Park," although discussions might go on "while the fence is up anyway." His principal Vice Chancellor, in an interview reported on May 22, stated that the University had not turned down a negotiating committee.

He also noted–and this was after the helicopter attack that "the fence was necessary to permit the kind of rational discussion and planning that wasn't possible before." Once more the faculty chairman had to protest that he had not been informed of meetings between the Administration and representatives of the People's Park and that the Chancellor had consistently ignored the committee's recommendations. However, the principal Vice Chancellor had an explanation for this lack of consultation: "I guess that's because the Chancellor didn't want him to get chewed up by this thing."

Why did the making of a park provoke such a desolating response? The bureaucratic nature of the multiversity and its disastrous consequences for education are by now familiar and beyond dispute. So, too, is the web of interdependence between it and the dominant military, industrial, and political institutions of our society. These explain much about the response of the University to the absurd, yet hopeful, experiment of People's Park.

What needs further comment is the increasingly ineffectual quality of the University's responses, particularly when its organizational apparatus attempts to cope with what is spontaneous, ambiguous, and disturbingly human. It is significant that the Berkeley Administration repeatedly expressed irritation with the failure of the Park people to "organize" a "responsible committee" or to select "representatives" who might "negotiate." The life styles and values of the Park people were forever escaping the categories and procedures of those who administer the academic plant.

Likewise the issue itself: the occupants of the Park wanted to use the land for a variety of projects, strange but deeply natural, which defied customary forms and expectations, whereas, at worst, the University saw the land as something to be fenced, soil-tested, processed through a score of experts and a maze of committees, and finally encased in the tight and tidy form of a rational design. At best, the most imaginative use of the land which the University could contemplate was as a "field-experiment station" where faculty and graduate students could observe their fellow beings coping with their "environment." In brief, the educational bureaucracy, like bureaucracies elsewhere, is experiencing increasing difficulty, because human life is manifesting itself in forms which are unrecognizable to the mentality of the technological age.

This suggests that part of the problem lies in the very way bureaucracies perceive the world and process information from it. It was this "bureaucratic epistemology" which largely determined how the University responded to the People's Park. Bureaucracy is both an expression of the drive for rationality and predictability and one of the chief agencies in making the world ever more rational and predictable, for the bureaucratic mode of knowing and behaving comes to constitute the things known and done themselves.

Now this rational form of organizing human efforts employs a conception of knowledge which is also rational in specific ways (cf. Kenneth Keniston's analysis in *The Uncommitted: Alienated Youth in American Society*, 1967, pp. 253-272). The only legitimate instrument of knowledge is systematic cognition, and the only acceptable mode of discourse is the cognitive mode. Other paths to knowledge are suspect. Everything tainted with the personal, the subjective, and the passionate is suppressed, or dismissed as prejudice or pathology. A bureaucrat who based his decisions upon, say, intuition, dialectical reason, empathic awareness, or even common sense, would be guilty of misconduct.

The bureaucratic search for "understanding" does not begin in wonder, but in the reduction of the world to the ordinary and the manageable. In order to deal with the world in the cognitive mode, the world must first be approached as an exercise in "problem-solving." To say there is a problem is to imply there is a solution; and finding the solution largely means devising the right technique. Since most problems are "complex," they must be broken down by bureaucrats into their component parts before the right solution can be found. Reality is parsed into an ensemble of discrete though related parts, and each part is assigned to the expert specially qualified to deal with that part. Wholes can appear as nothing more than assemblages of parts, just as a whole automobile is an assemblage of parts. But in order for wholes to be broken into parts, things that are dissimilar in appearance and quality must be made similar.

This is done by abstracting from the objects dealt with those aspects as though they were the whole. Abstraction and grouping by common attributes require measuring tools that yield comparable units for analysis: favorite ones are units of money, time, space, and power; income, occupation, and party affiliation. All such measurements and comparisons subordinate qualitative dimensions, natural context, and unique and variable properties to the common, stable, external, and reproducible. This way of thinking becomes real when campus administrators define "recreation" in fixed and restrictive terms so that it may accord with the abstract demands of "lead-time." In a way Hegel might barely recognize, the Rational becomes the Real and the Real the Rational.

When men treat themselves this way, they increasingly become this way, or they desperately try to escape the "mind-forged manacles," as Blake calls them, of the bureaucratic mentality and mode of conduct. In the broadest view, these two trends increasingly dominate the advanced states of our day. On the one side, we see the march toward uniformity, predictability, and the attempt to define all variety as dissent and then to force dissent into the "regular channels"—toward that state whose model citizen is Tocqueville's "industrious sheep," that state whose only greatness is its collective power.

On the other side we see an assertion of spontaneity, self-realization, and do-your-own-thing as the sum and substance of life and liberty. And this assertion, in its extreme form, does approach either madness or infantilism, for the only social institutions in which each member is really free to do his own thing are Bedlam and the nursery, where the condition may be tolerated because there is a keeper with ultimate control over the inmates. The opposing forces were not quite that pure in the confrontation over the People's Park, but the University and public officials nearly managed to make them so. That they could not do so is a comforting measure of the basic vitality of those who built the Park and who have sacrificed to preserve it.

But this still does not account for the frenzy of violence which fell on Berkeley. To understand that, we must shift focus.

Clark Kerr was perceptive when he defined the multiversity as "a mechanism held together by administrative rules and powered by money." But it is important to understand that the last few years in the University have seen more and more rules and less and less money. The money is drying up because the rules are being broken. The rules are being broken because University authorities, administrators and faculty alike, have lost the respect of very many of the students. When authority leaves, power enters—first in the form of more and tougher rules, then as sheer physical force, and finally as violence, which is force unrestrained by any thought of healing and saving, force whose aim is to cleanse by devastation.

Pressed from above by politicians and from below by

students, the University Administration simultaneously imposes more rules and makes continual appeals to the faculty for more support in its efforts to cope with permanent emergency. It pleads with the faculty for more "elbow room," more discretionary space in which to make the hard decisions needed when money runs short and students run amuck. That same Administration is right now conducting time-and-motion studies of faculty work and "productivity." Simultaneously, both faculty and Administration make spasmodic efforts to give the students some voice in the governance of the institution. But those are always too little, too late, too grudging.

Besides, as soon as the students get some power, unseemly things happen. Admit the blacks on campus and they demand their own autonomous department. Give the students limited power to initiate courses and they bring in Eldridge Cleaver and Tom Hayden. The faculty sees student initiative as a revolting mixture of Agitprop and denial of professional prerogatives. The Administration sees it as a deadly threat to its own precarious standing within the University and before the public. The politicians see it as concession to anarchy and revolution. The result is more rules and less trust all around—more centralization, bureaucratization, and force on one side, more despair and anger on the other.

Under these conditions, the organized system must strive to extend its control and reduce the space in which spontaneous and unpredictable actions are possible. The subjects, on the other hand, come to identify spontaneity and unpredictability with all that is human and alive, and rule and control with all that is inhuman and dead. Order and liberty stand in fatal opposition. No positive synthesis can emerge from this dialectic unless those who now feel themselves pushed out and put down are admitted as full participants. But that is not happening. More and more, we are seeing in this country a reappearance of that stage in the breakdown of political societies where one segment of the whole–in this case still the larger segment–determines to dominate by force and terror other segments which reject and challenge its legitimacy.

This dynamic largely accounts for the crushing violence and terror that hit Berkeley. When spontaneity appeared in People's Park, it was first met by a restatement of the rules governing possession and control of land. When that restatement did not have the desired effect, the University failed to take the next step dictated by rule-governed behavior–seeking an injunction. Nor did it take the step which would have acknowledged itself as being in a political situation–talking on a plane of equality and acting in a spirit of generosity with the other parties. Instead, it regressed immediately to the use of physical measures. In the eyes of the Administration, the building of People's Park was an "unjustified aggression," and the right of self-defense was promptly invoked.

Once force was called into play, it quickly intensified, and the University cannot evade its share of responsibility for what followed. He who wills the end wills the means; and no University official could have been unaware of the means necessary to keep that fence standing. But the administrators did not quite understand that their chosen agents of force, the police, would not limit their attention only to the students and street-people, who were expendable, but would turn against the University and the city as well.

Ronald Reagan reached Sacramento through Berkeley because, in the eyes of his frightened and furious supporters, Berkeley is daily the scene of events that would have shocked Sodom and revolutionary Moscow. All this came into intense focus in the behavior of the cops who were on the scene.

The police were numerous and armed with all the weapons a fertile technology can provide and an increasingly frightened citizenry will permit. Their superiority of force is overwhelming, and they are convinced they could "solve the problem" overnight if they were permitted to do it their own way: one instant crushing blow, and then license for dealing with the remaining recalcitrants. All the troublemakers are known to the police, either by dossier and record or by appearance and attitude. But the police are kept under some restraints, and those restraints produce greater and greater rage.

The rage comes from another source as well. Demands for a different future have been welling up in this society for some years now, and while those demands have not been unheard they have gone unheeded. Vietnam, racism, poverty, the degradation of the natural and man-made environment, the bureaucratization of the academy and its active collaboration with the military and industrial state, unrepresentative and unreachable structures of domination–all these grow apace. It seems increasingly clear to those who reject this American future that the forces of "law and order" intend to defend it by any means necessary. It becomes increasingly clear to the forces of law and order that extreme means will be necessary, and that the longer they are delayed the more extreme they will have to be.

Those two futures met at People's Park. It should be clear that what is happening this time is qualitatively different from 1964 and the Free Speech Movement. The difference in the amount of violence is the most striking, but this is largely a symptom of underlying differences. In 1964, the issues centered around questions of civil liberties and due process within the University. The issues now are political in the largest sense.

The appearance of People's Park raised questions of property and the nature of meaningful work. It raised questions about how people can begin to make a livable environment for themselves; about why both the defenders and critics of established authority today agree that authority can be considered only in terms of repression, never in terms of genuine respect and affection. These questions cannot be evaded. Those who honestly and courageously ask them are not imperiling the general happiness but are working for the common redemption.

It is increasingly clear that legitimate authority is declining in the modern state. In a real sense, "law and order" *is* the basic question of our day. This crisis of legitimacy has been visible for some time in just about all of the nonpolitical sectors of life—family, economy, religion, education—and is now spreading rapidly into the political realm. The gigantic and seemingly impregnable organizations that surround and dominate men in the modern states are seen by more and more people to have at their center not a vital principle of authority, but a hollow space, a moral vacuum. Increasingly, among the young and the rejected, obedience is mainly a matter of lingering habit or expediency or necessity, but not a matter of conviction and deepest sentiment.

The groups who are most persistently raising these questions are, of course, white middle-class youth and the racial and ethnic minorities. The origins of protest are different in the two cases: the former have largely seen through the American Dream of meaning in power and wealth and have found it a nightmare; the latter have been pushed aside and denied even the minimal goods of the Dream. But the ends of the protest are remarkably similar: both are fighting against distortions and denials of their humanity. Both reject the programmed future of an America whose only imperative now seems to be: more.

The people who built the Park (there will be more People's Parks, more and more occasions for seemingly bizarre, perverse, and wild behavior) have pretty much seen through the collective ideals and disciplines that have bound this nation together in its conquest of nature and power. Having been victimized by the restraints and authorities of the past, these people are suspicious of all authorities and most collective ideals. Some of them seem ready to attempt a life built upon no other ideal than self-gratification. They sometimes talk as though they had found the secret which has lain hidden through all the past ages of man: that the individual can live fully and freely with no authority other than his desires, absorbed completely in the development of all his capacities except two–the capacity for memory and the capacity for faith.

No one can say where this will lead. Perhaps new prophets will appear. Perhaps the old faith will be reborn. Perhaps we really shall see the new technological Garden tended by children–kind, sincere innocents, barbarians with good hearts. The great danger at present is that the established and the respectable are more and more disposed to see all this as chaos and outrage. They seem prepared to follow the most profoundly nihilistic denial possible, which is the denial of the future through denial of their own children, the bearers of the future.

In such times as these, hope is not a luxury but a necessity. The hope which we see is in the revival of a sense of shared destiny, of some common fate which can bind us into a people we have never been. Even to sketch out that fate one must first decide that it does not lie with the power of technology or the stability of organizational society. It lies, instead, in something more elemental, in our common fears that scientific weapons may destroy all life; that technology will increasingly disfigure men who live in the city, just as it has already debased the earth and obscured the sky; that the "progress" of industry will destroy the possibility of interesting work; and that "communications" will obliterate the last traces of the varied cultures which have been the inheritance of all but the most benighted societies.

If hope is to be born of these despairs it must be given political direction, a new politics devoted to nurturing life and work. There can be no political direction without political education, yet America from its beginnings has never confronted the question of how to care for men's souls while helping them to see the world politically. Seeing the world politically is preparatory to acting in it politically; and to act politically is not to be tempted by the puerile attraction of power or to be content with the formalism of a politics of compromise. It is, instead, a politics which seeks always to discover what men can share—and how what they share can be enlarged and yet rise beyond the banal.

People's Park is not banal. If only the same could be said of those who build and guard the fences around all of us.

IV
Education and The Technological Society

This and the next essay are not about Berkeley, though, no doubt, they are informed by the authors' Berkeley experience. Here we discuss powerlessness and revolution, developing at some length the themes briefly treated in the Introduction. *The essay also discusses the devastating effects of the technological culture on higher education, and proposes that that culture itself be made the central problem area of a reformed educational focus.*

OCTOBER 9, 1969

As this is being written, the colleges and universities are digging in for another round of campus troubles. Since the outbreak at Berkeley in 1964, the campuses have become a problem of national concern and, despite the many diagnoses, a matter of puzzlement. Although the head of one major university, responding to a US senator's question whether greater financial aid might not solve the universities' ills, remarked that he knew of no difficulty which would be worsened by more money, the puzzlement remains. Most educators and public officials agree that higher education is in deep financial trouble, but no one believes that lack of funds has produced student unrest, even though it may contribute to the conflicts over black and ethnic studies.

American politicians are not at their best when confronting problems which elude a financial solution, and it was only natural that they should fall back to other familiar positions. The first consisted of forcing the campus problems into legal categories from which, *presto*, they emerged as issues of rule violation and laxity in law enforcement. The obvious solution was to withdraw government aid from disaffected students and to warn the colleges and universities that they would suffer financial loss if they continued to be soft on law and order. The second position was equally predictable: trace the problems to an international Communist conspiracy, and then prove the allegation by introducing hostile witnesses, in this instance, some SDS types and a few Yippies.

Although it is likely that higher penalties will tend to discourage campus protests by raising the material and psychic costs to the activists, it is unlikely that such measures will prove to be of more than symbolic significance–interesting testimony to the ways our decision-makers perceive the problem within a framework of public outrage and private anxiety. President Nixon himself has expressed private worry that student discontents might persist even if the Vietnam war ended, which has the merit, at least, of leaving open the possibility of discussing the state of the campuses in other than the conventional terms of public policy. For it may be that we are experiencing a profound crisis in the liberal psyche, broader yet similar to that expressed by John Stuart Mill:

> Suppose that all your objects in life were real-

> ized, that all the changes in institutions and opinions which you are looking forward to could be completely effected at this very instant: would this be a great joy and happiness to you? And an irrepressible self-consciousness answered, "No!" At this my heart sank within me: the whole foundation on which my life was constructed fell down.

Suppose no Vietnam, no racial tensions, no poverty. . . .

Perhaps, then, we might think of the student problem, not as a policy question, but as a symbolic fact, as a state of affairs intimating a more general disorder.

Recall the remarkable quality of Academic Commencement, 1969. Normally commencement is an amiable time, when relatives, friends, and dignitaries gather to honor the graduating students and distinguished recipients of honorary degrees. But last June it was a time of high tension. Administrators and faculty prayed that the ceremonies might be completed without interruption by dissidents or militants. Parents looked on in shock and disbelief at the dress, deportment, and rhetoric of their offspring. The truly remarkable feature of commencement, however, was not the threat of disruption by the young, but the abdication and anxiety of the old. The President of the United States went near no major college or university. He chose, instead, to appear first at a junior college in South Dakota, where he dedicated the Karl Mundt Library and denounced student troublemakers, and then at the Air Force Academy in Colorado, where he affirmed that patriotism was still the highest virtue and pledged to defend the military against its domestic critics.

Customarily, commencement is a time when notable figures from public and private life invite their youthful audiences into the adult world and seek to describe its promise. But this year, all across the land, and in all manner of academic institutions, student speakers dominated the proceedings, telling the adults what was wrong with the world and what the new generation intended to do about it. They rejected both the austere past symbolized by Dakota and the cold war anticommunism of Karl Mundt, and the lethal and bleak technological future of the Air Force Academy. They insisted that the world was now theirs, and had to be understood in their terms.

The June events signified a reversal of the rites of passage and a redefinition of the rituals of rebellion. Despite that, they have now been nearly forgotten.

One reason why the events of June were soon forgotten is that the modes of interpreting campus troubles have become fixed within a certain pattern. Placed within that pattern, the June days seemed disturbing, but not surprising. For nearly a half-dozen years now the language and imagery of revolution have been used to describe and analyze events on the campuses—revolt, rebellion, student power, violence, and the like. Once this framework is set, a host of historical associations related to the great revolutions of the past arises, inflating the fears of the threatened and swelling the dreams of the hopeful. Believing themselves in the midst of revolution, both sides relax their inhibitions about violence.

Bacon once remarked that "even if men went mad all after the same fashion, they might agree one with another well enough." If political and campus officials and large numbers of students agree that they are locked in revolutionary struggle and strive to act accordingly, it is idle to say that they have misunderstood their situation. But it is worth asking, nonetheless, whether inherited notions of revolution are not anachronistic and hence a source of confusion for all parties.

Most of our ideas and images are still shaped by revolutions which happened in pre-industrial societies where differentials of wealth, power, and privilege were deeply and hopelessly etched, and where a small and visible ruling class on the top oppressed and exploited the masses on the bottom. The revolutions of France, Russia, and China were directed against the long historical past and its persistence into the present. Today, any lucid discussion of revolution in the advanced states must begin with the fact of technological society, not with ideas fashioned to analyze traditional societies. It must ask whether that fact does not by itself alter the sense in which a revolution is a meaningful possibility; whether social evils do not therefore acquire a novel form; and whether the marks of oppression are not to be sought among groups very different from the oppressed classes described in the classical literature of revolution.

The main feature of technological society is not merely rapid change, but, as its admirers have said, creative destruction. It not only destroys habits, beliefs, and institutions inherited from the past, but those which were created only yesterday. In a society where memory is an irritant because it impedes progress, concepts like "tradition" or categories like "the past" are mostly meaningless. To revolt against such a society means striking against the fluid present rather than against the burdensome past. It means, too, that instead of struggling, as revolutionists usually have, against societies which seemed incapable of moving and growing, today's revolutionist is in the absurd position of protesting against a society in constant movement and capable of promising everything, from the abolition of poverty to the abolition of death—either as a penalty or as a disease.

Talk about "revolution on the campus" is pathetic or mythological, for not only does it overlook the hard fact of technological society, but it also exaggerates the revolutionary potential of the campus. Because universities and colleges are vital to the economy and culture of technological society and because they exercise power over their own members, one may be deluded into believing that they are instrumentalities of power, and hence bases for revolution. Sometimes universities and colleges are able to exercise influence over other parts of society, but by most criteria of power they are weak. As potential centers of revolution they are hopeless, for there is little power to mobilize.

The manifest discontents and chronic disorders on the campuses are important, but their importance is distorted if they are viewed as revolutionary cells in a body politic vulnerable to the classic disorders of revolution. The condition of the campuses is significant because the campus represents the most advanced state of our society, not its most oppressed. It is where the knowledge explosion is happening, where the discontents with our racial, urban, and foreign policies are continuously aired and publicized, and where all manner of experiments are being lived by the new generation. Although student activists are apt to describe students as the "new proletariat" or simply as "niggers," their plight is significant not because they are oppressed but because they are corrupted.

Student discontent first broke out in the economically most advanced and affluent society (something which has been overlooked by social scientists who have warned of the impending "Latin Americanization of the universities"). Most of the trouble and violence has occurred at the most prestigious institutions. Except for the recent outbreaks by blacks and their "Third World" allies, the rebels have come from comfortable, professional, middle-class and upper middle-class families.

These are familiar facts, but the conclusion from them is what matters: if a revolutionary condition exists on the nation's campuses, it represents a protest by the middle class against the middle class. Or more pointedly, it is a condition created because the middle class has turned against its world and against its own values. How little similarity there is between the politics of the students and classical revolutionary situations is evident in the intense and almost universal hostility of the working classes and rural populations toward the students. The hatred of the "masses" is stirred by the abrasive politics on campus and by the casual sexuality, drug experimentation, and general slovenliness of the students. It is kept in motion by the continuous spectacle of the sons and daughters of those who have made it in America and who now defile those values of work, achievement, and upward mobility which sustain the city worker and the people of the small towns and rural areas. To claim that the workers and farmers of America are the victims of false consciousness is to miss the main point. What is being expressed on the campuses is a post-Marxian phenomenon, an attempt at change initiated from above and opposed to the aspirations, grievances, and values of those below the middle classes in the social hierarchy. It is, moreover, an attempt at revolution which dare not go into the streets, the factories, and (increasingly) the ghettos.

If the state of the campuses is more reflective of a middle-class revolt than of a revolutionary situation, then the relative ineffectiveness of the students may reveal something important about the possibilities of fundamental change in a liberal, affluent, and technologically advanced society. Tocqueville's conjecture that among democratic nations "great intellectual and political revolutions will become more difficult and less frequent than is supposed" now seems confirmed. A society capable of producing floods of consumer goods, of supporting high levels of employment or subsidizing those it cannot employ, of practicing a form of politics in which organized groups gain some material satisfaction most of the time, and of providing endless varieties of entertainment and distraction is a difficult target to attack. Such a society lends itself more to "targets of opportunity" than to frontal assaults, e.g., poverty, discrimination, inadequate housing, and exploited fruit-pickers.

The dominant groups of this society are, from the revolutionary point of view, elusive. They prefer the politics of influence and indirect power, rarely flaunt their privileges, and are open to new recruits. It has been a century since they have told the public where it can go. The lack of clearly defined enemies is tacitly recognized in the vocabulary of the rebels: the use of words like "dissent" and of actions like "protest," "resistance," and "demonstration" are an admission that they are reduced to seeking targets of opportunity within a generally benevolent system. Because the liberal, affluent, technological society is characteristically bland, accommodating, and good-natured, it renders the revolutionary powerless, allowing him to act out, outrageously if he wishes, his subversive impulses, encourages him to theatrical revolution, which means that he can shock but never destroy.

The affability of the managers of technological society

is encouraged by something more than the fact that they preside over an economy which supplies them, as no other ruling group has ever been supplied, with a generous margin or surplus so that concessions are always possible and mistakes always corrigible. What they have in addition is the enormous power—also without historical precedent—which accrues to those who control a society of consumers, a power owing as much to the powerlessness of the subjects as to the instrumentalities of the rulers. In all previous societies, powerlessness was the consequence of deprivation: deprivation of rights, privileges, property, work, education. Although pockets of material deprivation still exist, the main source of powerlessness is not deprivation but consumption. Technological society lives by consumption, and its members live for it. They allow the quality and tempo of their lives to be set by the changing requirements of technology. They above all acquiesce happily in the reduction of control over the quality and intensity of personal experience which is one of the fruits of technology.

Think of the American who comes to Yosemite in a camper truck with a boat on top, a motorcycle strapped to the front, and a power-boat trailered to the rear. He thinks he has expanded his range of action and his powers of enjoyment, whereas he has really become the prisoner of his technology, restricted to where it can take him and what it can bring him. He suffers a reduction in personal power and experience even while thinking he has extended them. It is instructive that in the same state of nature the sworn enemy of the camper trucker should end in the same state of powerlessness. Deep in the wilderness one may meet a bearded and beaded hippie, totally stoned, incapacitated from encountering nature on its terms. He has renounced the powerlessness of active consumption for the powerlessness of passive consumption.

The powerlessness of the many forms the larger setting for the powerlessness of the campus rebels. The dominant groups in our society do not fear the latter; on the contrary, they find much that is charming and usable in their dress, idiom, and eternal youthfulness–so much so that constant efforts are made to absorb the culture of the young. It may come out wrong, sometimes emerging as *Playboy* culture and commercial advertising. Yet, as we know from recent accounts, the gap between Mrs. Luce and the rebels is not always great. What does alarm the elites, and helps to explain their willingness to support harsh measures against the campuses, is the possibility that the antics of the rebels will intensify and ignite the deep-seated fears and hatreds of broad sectors of the population: urban workers of recent foreign origin, small-town America, and the less sophisticated middle classes in the South, Middle West, Southwest, and Southern California.

The dominant groups *do* fear polarization, but they fear one of the polarities–the student rebels–not so much for what it represents as for the forces it may activate. They fear the other for what it does represent. It brings reminders, often unattractive, of what technological society is always trying to forget and to destroy: its past–a past in which work, self-denial, simplicity, and physical strength were celebrated. Whereas the technological elites can share with the rebels a common fascination for electronic marvels and for the endless movement which modern communications and transportation allow, and can enjoy in private the pleasures which the rebels flaunt in public, those same elites are repelled by honkies,

Southerners, and citizens of Orange County. But because they know that the real threat to technological society comes from those who are frightened and confused by incessant change, they are willing to sanction, perhaps reluctantly, firm measures against those who are hip, mod, cool, and really plugged into the future.

The fundamental malady of technological society, then, is the nearly universal sense of powerlessness, disguised as consumption and maintained by rising expectations. That sense of powerlessness is expressed in various ways: in the rage and confusion of the working and lower-middle classes; in the aimlessness of the middle-class hippie; in the despair of the poor and the anger of the blacks; in the fear and harshness of the American Gothics who rallied first to Goldwater and then to Wallace.

Among the many causes which promote our common futility there is one that has gone relatively unnoticed. We may be the first people to experience what it means to live in accordance with the fundamental postulates of the scientific and technological credo. It is one thing to talk, as philosophers and scientists have done for a century, about the differences between scientific beliefs and moral, religious, and political beliefs; about the objective status of the one and the subjective status of the other; about how the one is grounded in empirical realities and the other in prejudice, superstition, or metaphysics; and about how the one gives us power over nature and the future, while the other gives us only solace for our ignorance.

It is quite another thing when an entire society attempts to shape its life by scientific and technical knowledge, making that knowledge the very foundation for the continuance and the security of society, and encouraging its pursuit even to the point of sacrificing the welfare and shattering the memories and hopes of many of its citizens. It is quite another thing because that knowledge is, by the admission of its exponents, silent on the questions of how a man should live and what he should choose. Those who have interpreted the meaning, presuppositions, and methods of scientific and technical knowledge have insisted that it cannot prescribe ends. They have also asserted that other forms of knowing whose business it is to traffic in "values" lack the characteristics of genuine knowledge, e.g., empirical verification, quantifiability, even rationality.

Once the scientific culture takes hold, there is a scramble to emulate it and thereby avoid the stigma of inferiority; hence its spread to the social studies, history, and the humanities. The end result is the divorce between knowledge and values symbolized by the underlying agreement between the techno-scientist and the hippie, the one declaring that values are subjective preferences, the other mumbling, "Man, I'm only doing my thing." The end result signifies that values are no longer shareable as knowledge, and hence one gets only their functional equivalents: sensation, feeling, spectacle.

But if it is in the nature of the techno-scientific culture to render values private and unshareable, perhaps there is still hope. Perhaps there is one important value crucial to that culture and yet a value to which all can subscribe and even share, the value of knowledge itself.

Knowledge permeates the whole ethos and structure of technological society. This is what mainly distinguishes it from previous forms of society. Consequently, higher education plays a vital role. Its institutions have become the foundation of a society based on scientific knowledge. We must then ask two questions concerning the universities and colleges. Are they succeeding in making knowledge something that can truly be shared? Are they realizing the goal of making knowledge power and hence a means of overcoming human powerlessness?

At first glance it appears that the university has the prerequisites of a community held together by the active sharing of knowledge. Many of the conditions one would want to postulate seem fulfilled. For some time now public universities have been committed to opening their doors to a wide variety of groups and classes. Along with the private institutions, they are now making a serious effort to enroll sizable numbers of students from racial and ethnic groups. Within tolerable limits, the communities of higher education are open; and, despite mounting costs, education is relatively cheap and available. Beyond these and other material conditions conducive to sharing knowledge, there have been the great changes in the nature of knowledge, typified by modern science, which also seem to promote communal ends. Of the many things that might be said to characterize the modern ideal of knowledge, these are the least disputable: it is rational, secular, empirical, cumulative, and public. No secret mysteries, no fixed dogma, no priesthood.

Thus modern knowledge appears uniquely designed to be the stuff from which communities of scholars and students might be formed. In addition, the modern idea of knowledge has promised to help men to a fuller measure of personal freedom, liberating them from ignorance and superstition, and enlarging the efficacy and power of the individual. Unlike those who had trafficked in metaphysics, theology, aesthetics, and the like, the modern man would know something that could be applied directly to the world. He could be equipped to move into the world, confident of his ability to make a place for himself where what *he* did would make a difference in shaping his life.

Yet when we look at what the modern ideal of knowledge has become in the university, we find that at every turn it threatens to diminish what it had promised to enlarge: freedom, efficacy, and sharing. The modern ideal is summed up in the slogan about the "knowledge explosion," which the universities have done so much to detonate. So great is the proliferation of knowledge that the problem now is how to retrieve it from the swelling data banks where it is stored. Realistically, the "knowledge explosion" means that a few know a great deal about how nature and society "work," while the rest of us are about as ignorant as we have always been. Further, as knowledge has become increasingly refined, it becomes more inaccessible to the many, more esoteric, more removed from the world of common experience.

Comparable effects have also been produced in the life of the university by the pursuit of knowledge as a form of power. Repeating the pattern of the outside world, a few university men enjoy great power, while the many are about as powerless as they have always been, perhaps more so. Power within the university depends upon the demands of the "knowledge-market" outside. Those in the university who have knowledge which is in demand, or, equally important, know how to organize those who do have it, come to have superior power and influence. Their superiority is exhibited in countless "special arrangements," higher salaries, lower teaching loads, more research support, more spacious accommodations, and more influence in university councils.

All of this is obvious. It is necessary only to draw the

obvious conclusion: the distinction between university and society, the enduring effort of universities to develop a life and culture different from that of society—an effort which began with Plato's Academy and continued into recent times—is now a distinction without a difference. If anything of a difference remains it is a consequence of the reversal which has taken place in the relationships between university and society. Broadly speaking, from the sixteenth century to the end of the nineteenth, universities were frequently criticized for failing to assimilate important types of knowledge, such as modern languages, newer forms of mathematics and science, and various practical arts. In our century, however, it is the other way round. Society is constantly required to adapt to the knowledge being developed in the universities, knowledge not only in the natural sciences and engineering, but in economics, psychology, and sociology as well.

These changes have registered their severest effects upon undergraduate education, especially at the large public universities. Today, undergraduate education is a shambles. Traditionally it has had the task of general education, of defining and transmitting the knowledge appropriate to a "well-educated" or "cultivated" man. When a civilization reaches a fair degree of self-consciousness and self-definition it embodies in a formal curriculum those values which it regards as essential to the best intellect and sensibility: the Greek Academy; the medieval *trivium* and *quadrivium*; the liberal-humanistic curriculum of the nineteenth century.

Moreover, in those earlier societies possession of the knowledge imparted through the college succeeded fairly well in equipping men for understanding themselves and their social orders and for taking positions of influence in church, state, and society. And since virtually all the educated shared a common fund of knowledge, college education enabled all those who had it to converse among themselves about the questions that mattered.

Merely to say these things is to see immediately how far we have moved from them. While all of the older conceptions of the content and purposes of undergraduate education still linger on in more or less mutilated form, nobody is very certain of their utility—or, as it is called today, "relevance." Certainly, they provide the stuff of commencement day addresses and college catalogue prose, but few will still argue that they provide the knowledge that leads to social power and influence. Nor is anyone really convinced that the liberal arts curriculum teaches values and molds character. About the strongest claim made for education in the arts and humanities today is that the knowledge so gained can enrich one's leisure time: education to solve the "problem of leisure"; and leisure here means recreation, not the fullest use of one's capacities.

The fact is, we simply do not know the form of the highest general culture appropriate to contemporary, largely post-industrial society. Whatever that general culture might come to be and mean, it certainly will not merely be what it always has been. Most colleges occupy the undergraduate years with a kind of pre-professional training and specialization, or a pedantic and uncertain humanism, or an uneasy compromise between the two—some "breadth" courses, followed by concentration in a "major." The result saddens the best teachers, maddens the best students, and gladdens no one.

But the undergraduate curriculum will remain motley and infirm until the colleges decide what those vulnerable years in the lives of the young are for, and what they are not for. The most powerful emerging tendencies are either treating the undergraduate student as a candidate for graduate or professional school, or arranging things so that the student can have the greatest possible latitude for personal search and experiment. Both tendencies, of course, intensify intellectual fragmentation and pluralistic ignorance, leading to privatization rather than to genuine sharing of knowledge and experience. Once again the extremes produce weakness and lead to a society of disconnected particulars. On the one side, increasing professionalization, on the other, a growing tendency to let students go their own ways. Each tendency hurries the student toward his own cocoon.

Compared to the desperate confusions of undergraduate life, the higher reaches of the higher learning—graduate and professional schools and advanced research centers—appear peaceful and well-ordered. A closer look reveals currents which conceal weakness beneath professionalization, atomization beneath organization, powerlessness beneath power.

The proliferation of specialized knowledge, in addition to the availability of research funds, in addition to the tendency to inflate into "professional" status occupations that are really little more than fairly highly skilled jobs, has turned the modern large university into a bewilderingly complex collection of special institutes, centers, bureaus, and schools. These units occupy a semi-autonomous status within the university, enjoying their own budgets, governed by their own officers, adopting their own standards for staff and student performance, and largely oriented toward constituencies outside the university. The resulting centrifugal forces are ungovernably strong, and increasingly the university becomes a holding company with only nominal control over the agencies which bear its name.

These tendencies are strengthened by the multiversitarian ideology of the university as the servant of society. Under this ideology, knowledge is seen as the single most important "growth factor" in modern economies, and universities, as the leading producers within the knowledge industry, become indispensable to all the other productive agencies of society. Universities have always in some sense served society. But never has service been so mundanely conceived or so promiscuously offered as by the modern multiversity.

The precondition of university service to society is professional education. The natural locus of that education is the graduate departments. One expects to find a degree of professionalism in graduate study, but what is now of concern is the tendency to substitute specialization for professionalism and to extend an inflated professionalism into areas of higher education where it does not belong. At its core, the idea of a profession involves a body of knowledge and technique that can be codified, transmitted, and applied in standard ways to socially useful ends. A professional is one who has been certified by other professionals as being in possession of the prescribed knowledge. Specialization as such is not the basic mark of the professional: the lawyer in general practice is as much a professional as the one who specializes in tax law.

The Ph.D. degree most clearly displays the effects of specialization disguised as professionalism. It is no longer regarded as the badge of the man who has acquired competence in a body of knowledge which he wishes to profess to others, whose vocation is scholarship and the pursuit of significant truth, and who gives promise of intellectual creativity. In a growing number of fields, the degree is nothing more than a certification that a man has mastered a limited subject matter and certain techniques of work. The consequences are already apparent, and most are harmful: microspecialization of knowledge, narrowness of outlook, a growing inability to define intellectual significance in any terms other than those set by the techniques of research, and progressive disqualification for the task of teaching undergraduates. His growing expertise closes off much of his subject-field, while surrounding fields are *terrae incognitae*. His capacities for personal growth come to be defined in terms of growing technical mastery. But even this proves illusory: every field is now expected to be in "ferment," and hence the techniques acquired as a graduate student will be superseded in a brief time. The only hope left is that he may some day become a dean.

It remains to point out one general feature of the modern job and income structure that has an important bearing on present student discontent. In simpler and more stable eras, persons who went to college could usually make an early choice of career with fair confidence that the future would contain a place for them. Furthermore, those who went to college could count on a future that would bring them a fair measure of personal independence and social influence and prestige: even the schoolteacher was a figure of considerable standing in the small towns of yesterday. But today, with the vast increase in the college-educated population, these exceptions no longer hold. Furthermore, millions of the college-educated now hold jobs that are far below their skills and ability, and those jobs have all the features of industrial work save one—the need for muscle. The work is repetitive, narrow, and stunting.

The college-educated—including increasing numbers of those formally classified as professional—can no longer confidently look forward to places within the established occupational structure that will bring them independence, challenging work, and social influence. They can count on a fair measure of material comfort and security, but more and more young people are asking whether that is sufficient reward for the sacrifice of autonomy and growth. This long-range change in the shape of work is perhaps one of the basic factors underlying youthful discontent and protest. In often vague and poorly focused ways, students are demanding that education be something more than a union card to job security in the bureaucratic-technological society, where one's talents are exploited for the purposes of others, and where the worker has traded most of the dimensions of genuine freedom enjoyed by former educated and professional classes for clean clothes and comfortable working conditions. But the implementation of that rising demand will require radical changes in the occupational and organizational structure of the technological society itself.

Societies have always been, in part, organizations for the production of the nutrients of life, but modern societies are ruled as no others have ever been by the drive for production. Modern production is powerfully oriented toward consumption; and, since consumption is limitless, so too is production. But to produce something means to destroy something else. That is the dynamic of modern production: it must continue as long as there is anything left to destroy.

The evidence of the destructiveness is all around us, both in the realm of nature and in the realm of that "second nature" which is culture. Modern production has obscured the sun and the stars, and it has also made the cities unlivable. It chews up great forests and drinks whole lakes and rivers, and it consumes men's religions and traditions and makes nonsense of their notions of the aims of education. It periodically slays heaps of men in war, and it daily mangles the spirits of millions of others in meaningless labor. The only aim of the civilization is to grow, and to grow it must consume. As Ellul has shown, the process must run until it consumes those who think they run it—until man is absorbed into technique and process.

The great intellectual task of the present is the task of rethinking every aspect of technological civilization. That this civilization inherently moves toward self-destruction is now clear, and any radical rethinking must start from the premise that its manifest destructiveness will not be stopped by a broader distribution of the values or a more intensive application of the methods and processes which constitute and sustain the evil itself. If the universities were to dedicate themselves to this rethinking, then they would not only serve society in the most valuable way possible, but they might even save themselves.

This task will require more than the opening of the curriculum to miscellaneous "problem courses" on whatever happens to be interesting or bothering people at the moment—with the consequence that the problems of peace, race, poverty, and transcendental meditation all receive equal time. It will require something more of the scientists and technicians than stopping work for a "day of concern." It will require something more of the humanists than a deeper retreat into the sanctuary of ingeniously obscure research, while mumbling incantations about "higher values." What it will require is a new focus, and the courage to withdraw human and material resources from the subjects which have high value on the current market, reallocating them to the task of rediscovering and redefining the humanity and sociability which have become twisted and frustrated by the "single vision" of contemporary modes of organization and public purpose.

The task is in part critical: to examine what technological civilization has done to our language, literature, art, politics, and work. Partly it is retrospective: to expose the historical choices that were made by reference to the putative benefits of science and technology placed in the service of endless growth and power. That study must try to achieve a meaningful assessment of the gains and losses incurred by these choices. Partly it is creative: to reflect upon human history in all of its breadth and diversity in order to acquire the fullest comprehension of the range of human possibilities and, perhaps, a heightened awareness of the crisis which has estranged us from our humanity and our world.

We have preferred to call it a focus rather than a curriculum in order to emphasize the urgency of our condition. Technological civilization encompasses and influences all departments of knowledge, hence it is not just *a* problem: it is *the* problem. There is no subject more relevant, none so important for the renewal of hope for our species.

V
Where We Are Now

One of the defining features of the decade of the Sixties was the appearance of youth as a distinctive status and presence in American life. This essay surveys and assesses the impact of young people on mainstream American politics during the decade. That impact was surely great and, we think, on the whole salutary. The New Left opened many basic questions that had to be asked and brought needed vitality to American politics. At the same time, the inability of the political system to make use of this energy in generous ways, or to deal creatively with the issues raised by youth, can be measured by the price exacted from the young, a price paid in the coin of broken careers, self-destructive experiments, disrupted educations, even loss of liberty and life. The New Left is now dead, partly crushed by the weight of an increasingly repressive system, partly wrecked by its own inability to develop either a new radical theory beyond both liberalism and socialism or a conception of action coherent enough to sustain its members in a political vocation.

But if the New Left as such is dead, the political impulse among youth is not. The campus response to the invasion of Cambodia, which we shall discuss at some length in the Epilogue, *has surely proved that.*

MAY 7, 1970

On February 1, 1960, four neatly dressed freshman students from a Negro college took seats at the whites-only Woolworth's lunch counter in Greensboro, North Carolina, politely asked for coffee, and refused to leave until the store closed. Ten years and a thousand marches later, Fred Hampton lay dead in Chicago, the latest casualty in the police war against the Black Panthers. In early 1962, the Students for a Democratic Society adopted the Port Huron Statement, which argued that both "the liberal and socialist preachings of the past" were inadequate to the present, and pledged the formation of a "New Left" based in the universities and committed to the methods of "participatory democracy." On March 6, 1970, a few young members of that New Left, now divided and dispirited, accidentally obliterated themselves with their homemade bombs. The decade of the metaphorical "youth explosion" ended with a literal bang. One era had ended and another begun.

During the Sixties, the young achieved a distinctive status for themselves, a status almost as sharply defined as that of other accursed or blessed groups, such as blacks, Jews, Junkers, and right-wing deviationists. The young demanded and received recognition of their distinctiveness as a group bearings its own values, possessing a unique culture, and dedicated to its own ends. Youth made a deep impact on politics, education, fashion, art, and the consumer economy. The entire nation was aware of the new presence: a Gallup Poll of March, 1969, reported that campus disorders had replaced the Vietnam war as the primary concern of Americans.

Nowhere was the youth presence more visible than on the political scene, where it brought into being a phenomenon requiring a special name. Throughout most of our history, Americans, whether young or old, have not shown a great passion for politics. But the youth of the Sixties showed more political passion than any earlier generation, giving promise of a revitalization of American politics, perhaps even the birth of the American as a political man. The generation experimented with a rich variety of truly political actions and showed a genuine concern for public things, thereby reversing the long trend toward privatization. The young argued, sang, marched, organized, sat in, milled around, walked out, and disrupted. And always the system responded too little, too late, or not at all. Starting with the last half of the Sixties, the politics of the young grew more desperate and factional; and, since the Democratic Convention of 1968, more frantic, more clandestine, and more violent. Apparently fearing that political energy could not move the system, more and more of the young began to seek political substitutes in the illusions of potency provided by Woodstock, dynamite, or drugs.

It is now evident that the youthful politics of the Sixties is over. The mutilated bodies in the rubble of that Greenwich Village house speak loudly of desperation and exhaustion—of too many hopes and dreams wrecked, too much enthusiasm thwarted. The swift, savage years of the Sixties may come to be seen as the time when America said "no" to much of the best that was herself.

It is too early yet to assess the full impact of the youthful politics of the Sixties on the larger political system, but some things can be said.

Over the course of its first ten years, the New Left

failed to create the new radical theory beyond both liberalism and socialism which the Port Huron Statement had called for. Although the New Left gradually has moved away from the single-issue, basically reformist outlook of the early Sixties over toward a general indictment of the system, that movement was not powered or accompanied by an increasingly coherent and comprehensive theory. Rather, it is a mood, a feeling of rage and revulsion, which is increasingly impatient with theory, or even thought and argument. The anti-intellectualist strain which was present in the movement from the beginning has triumphed. Theory on the New Left is now reduced to the vulgar Marxism and Maoism of Progressive Labor, or to the Weatherman view of white radicals as a suicide squad providing cover for black urban guerrillas, the true vanguard of the revolution.

Nor was the New Left able to develop a conception of political action coherent and effective enough, over the long pull, to sustain its members in a political vocation—to answer the questions: What does a radical look like in American politics, and how does he define himself in action which goes beyond the episodic and theatrical? Even the heroes, the ego-ideals, of the New Left are drawn from Cuba and China, despite the fact that the only indisputable statement that can be made about any future American revolution is that it will not look at all like any foreign revolutions we have read about. To mistake the many sporadic outbursts and uprisings of the past decade for *the* American Revolution is to misunderstand the nature of the political system within which these events have occurred and to underestimate the capacity of that system to assimilate or to suppress anomalies.

Many modes of action have been tried by the New Left—civil rights work, community organizing, on-campus organizing, antidraft unions, factory organizing, political action as guerrilla theater, even electoral politics—but none offered a decisive lever for radical change. There are now few hopeful projects on the left, and the only lively alternative life styles seem to be Weatherman adventurism and the Yippie freakout. Maybe the only hopeful possibility for action—perhaps it was always the best one—is Rudi Dutschke's "long march through the existing institutions."

But that means that the New Left would have to become less a student and youth movement and more a radical political grouping drawn from and able to work within many sectors of society for many different but unspectacular goals. The goals chosen would be those with high potential for accentuating evident contradictions in particular institutions, thereby undermining their present structures and challenging their present policies.

The New Left, so far, has shown little taste for such patient and pedestrian strategies. New Left radicals, for example, despite their own argument that the knowledge industry is the key industry in advanced societies, never developed much in the way of a theory and practice of counter-education. The "Free Universities," for example, have accomplished little; and most student efforts toward radical experimentation within the established universities have been suppressed or assimilated. The campuses are quieter now, because their managers have raised the ante on disruption and become more efficient at suppression, because few new leaders have appeared in the New Left since the early Sixties, and also because people have learned that episodic outbursts, powered by indignation and hope but not sustained and directed by theory, are ineffective.

Despite these failings, the political impulses of the young during the Sixties have had decisive consequences for the larger political order. The young opened up many closed questions, forcing them into the arena of public controversy, and making it "safe" and politically profitable for the middle forces in American politics to adopt them as issues. Thus while the young have not stopped the Vietnam war, they have reduced its scope and changed its objectives. Not many years ago only a handful of public men dared to oppose the war. Now opposition is so respectable that any overt attempt to spread the conflict to Laos and Cambodia would encounter strong official and popular resistance. Furthermore, debate about the war has also opened the question of American imperialism and neocolonialism, a question closed in the public mind since the Spanish-American War.

Many other questions were opened to public debate by the young people of the Sixties: civil rights and racial justice; conscription and the impact of militarism on American life; the structure and content of higher education, and university complicity with the military and corporate establishments. The young radicals publicized the issues of impersonality and bureaucracy, and sensitized their peers to the subtlety and ubiquity of the modes of bureaucratic control. It was the young who offered a serious and widespread challenge, for the first time, to the values associated with technology, rationalism, objectivity, and bigness. And now the question of ecology has also been opened. (We shall return to this.)

The young opened all these questions, and made them safe for the middle. In order for the Muskies, McGoverns, and Fulbrights to criticize the Vietnam calamity with political safety, many of the young have been jailed or forced into exile or the underground. In order for civil rights and racial justice to become part of the nation's agenda, the young—black and white alike—have risked their careers and their lives. In order for the biases and hypocrisy of the legal system to become matters of public concern, and for the institution of the police to be seen as a political problem of the first order, the young have paid heavily in their freedom, security, and dignity.

In order for sexual mores to become more than a matter of polite discussion, the young have been driven to experiments in which they have taken on burdens and undergone experiences beyond their capacities. In order for the colleges and universities to reappraise the meaning of education, the young have had to disrupt their own educations and to pay the price in ignorance. In order for the ethic of technocracy and the cult of objectivity to be questioned, a whole generation had to blow its collective mind in self-experimentation.

What is fantastic about the politics of the Sixties is that this crazy compound of wild energy, bizarre experiments, and the large number of lives whose promise will never be fulfilled has all gone toward getting the moderates of America to address themselves to the problems which have been tearing the society apart. The young may not have radically altered the system, but they have probably saved it, though only at a terrible cost to themselves. This, apparently, is what it takes to move the system.

The impact of the young on the political order does not end with the list of issues opened and made safe for debate. There have been other, equally important consequences.

By insistent criticism, the New Left has also brought

into question the moral and democratic pretensions of many of the dominant institutions of this country. One must add, however, that the institutions themselves gave their radical enemies a lot of aid and comfort in this campaign. Certainly when Lyndon Johnson ran for the Presidency on promises of peace in Vietnam and then escalated the war, he did more than the New Left ever could to expose the mockeries of electoral democracy. Judge Hoffman's antics in Chicago did more to subvert the authority of the judicial system than defendant Hoffman ever dreamed was possible. Similar contributions were made by the faculties and managing directors of a dozen major universities.

Still, the basic fact is that the last decade has seen a profound "de-authorization" of many of the major institutions, and the New Left has contributed heavily to that phenomenon. Simultaneously feeding and feeding upon the animus against authority widespread among young people today, the New Left has contributed much to the present crisis of civic culture in America, a crisis which spans the whole range of civic obligations, from simple obedience to the law to the sacrifice of personal interests for the public good. America can no longer count on an instinctive patriotism among the young. One of the consequences of that may be a professional army, an institution which, historically, has been fatal to republics.

The coalition that has governed this land since 1932 is shattered. Even liberals now concede that the system has problems whose solutions will require more than incremental adjustments within an established frame. The fundamental structure of power has not changed, of course, but the balance of forces has shifted. Liberals no longer define the issues and set the general direction of affairs and policy. Rather, they respond to the forces of the left and right. More than that, the public mind is going through a historical shift of consciousness. On all sectors of the political spectrum, there is a growing doubt that the liberal myth and logic will dominate the American future. The New Left has been instrumental in this process—which is a way of saying that it did something that the conservatives have struggled unsuccessfully to do since 1932.

One final dimension in this brief assessment of the impact of the New Left. Social change has moved at such a rapid pace from the beginning of the Republic that responses to it have largely provided the stuff of American politics. Our political history shows a repeated pattern of groups and sections feeling left behind, pushed out, by the pace and content of social change. From the beginning, one or another "older America" has felt that it has lost the Republic, has been pushed out of its own place and left homeless. The Federalists were convinced that Jeffersonian republicanism meant the end of their world. The Civil War left the South with no acceptable future. Industrialism meant the death of rural and small-town America, and democracy seemed to the cultivated and respectable classes to mean the end of virtue and propriety altogether. White Anglo-Saxondom lost America to a motley host of strangers. The list could be extended, but each case exemplifies the pattern of an older America feeling itself robbed of both past and future by a new America. That pattern characterizes much of our political life, and largely accounts for the fact that most radical and reform movements in this country have offered a program of "forward to yesterday." A better future meant return to a better past.

The revolt of the New Left, combined with the cultural revolution of the Sixties, marked a reversal in this pattern. It was a revolt, not of those who were left behind, not of those who once had a place but were pushed out of it, but of those who felt that America never had a place for them. It was a revolt not of those who felt they could not transmit their legacy to the future, but of those who rejected the legacy which was offered them. It was a revolt of the young, who saw America not as a gift but as a burden, who refused the roles and identities prepared for them by their fathers, and who still feel themselves to be superfluous in the future which they are told is theirs. That is why New Left politics and the cultural revolution were in large part struggles for identity. That is also why the demands and the style of the young in this period were met with such bitter resistance. For the young rejected the gift, and you do not do that without earning the hatred of the giver. That is new in American politics, and it is one of the ways to state the defining impact of the New Left on the old system.

So there has been a difference, even a great difference. But underneath, it is possible to see forces within the system that seem implacable to change, ineluctably working out a logic deeper than the conscious intentions of either right or left. Nixon's State of the Union message of January 22, 1970, offers some clues to those forces, and perhaps shows the tendencies of the present and foreseeable future.

The President first celebrated the past and reminded us that we would soon commemorate our two hundredth anniversary. But he also spoke of the Seventies as a "time of new beginnings," requiring a "break with tradition."

He offered absolution from past failures: "We have heard a great deal of overblown rhetoric during the Sixties in which the word war has perhaps too often been used. The war on poverty, the war on misery, the war on disease, the war on hunger." The President then identified the real enemy and promised all-out war: "But if there is one area where the word war is appropriate it is in the fight against crime. We must declare and win the war against the criminal elements. . . ."

Then, without pausing to adjust his rhetoric or his conception of action, he announced his major theme: "Shall we make our peace with nature, and begin to make reparations for the damage we have done to our air, to our land and to our water?"

That the longest and most significant part of the speech was devoted to "the great question of the Seventies," the natural environment, was a recognition not only of the intrinsic importance of these problems but also of their great interest to the younger generation. As the President noted, the restoration of nature "is the cause of particular concern to young Americans. . . ."

By this move Nixon captured the issue which might allow for peace between the political system and the younger generation. Many months before the President made his overtures, youthful groups had been energetically spreading the news about nature. Some were ecstatic worshippers of the *Ur-Mutter*, others were engaged in establishing rural communes, and still others were popularizing scientific doctrines of ecology, warning against pollution and overpopulation, and staging "walks for life." By their own admission the new activists were abandoning the old issues.

"The fact is," one student leader declared, "the colleges just do not count." And, with varying degrees of candor, they were saying the same about racial issues, poverty, and war. In some half-conscious way, the younger generation had already begun to grope toward the accommodation which the President later offered. As a young writer in *Earth Times* put it, "It would be the ultimate cop-out to give all our money to the Black Panthers and then have them all die in twenty years because they couldn't drink the water." Most Panthers, it is safe to say, will not die of thirst.

As the President's speech made clear, the terms of the new consensus would have to be consistent with the logic of technological society. He promised both technological progress *and* a better environment. "The answer is not to abandon growth but to redirect it." The need was not to develop radically different ways of thinking about life but to develop "better ways of managing what we have." The environmental crisis was not cause for rethinking the implications of technology but for enlarging its uses. We must "turn toward ending congestion and eliminating smog the same inventive genius that created them in the first place." The "wonders of science" had only to be turned "to the service of man." In sum, an environmental version of the theme of gaining peace by waging war.

His ultimate vision was a uniquely American combination of scientific technology and the Protestant ethic. Our "debt to nature" requires that we "clean up our environment" which has been dirtied by "carelessness." In this way the society could reclaim its "birthright" of "clean air, clean water."

The young responded eagerly. On March 15 a gigantic teach-in was held at the University of Michigan to discuss the problems of environment. It was described by *The*

New York Times as "one of the most extraordinary 'happenings' ever to hit the great American heartland. . . ." In fact, it was all very familiar, from the $50,000 budget of the happening–$5,000 of which is said to have come from Dow Chemical–to the enthusiastic participation of "state officials . . . members of Congress, industry, labor, and several representatives of the Nixon Administration," and to the politician who beseeched the audience to "pressure" him and his fellow congressmen into passing environmental legislation. Thus was found the issue around which the hippies and the Hickels might unite.

This new preoccupation with the natural environment means that for the first time since the early Sixties, when civil rights agitation reached its crest, an issue exists which can connect the energies and ideals of the young to the policies and machinery of the system. Past controversies over the war, the draft, and educational reform sharply divided the young activists from their governors and elders. Now, on the broad ground of environment, they stand in common cause with the power elite. It is the kind of issue which is particularly appealing when the disappointments and abrasions of political encounters become too much, for it permits a full catharsis of moral indignation without seriously altering the structure of power or the logic of the system. Outrage can be directed against enemies whose evils are manifest, enemies who pollute and dirty, enemies who turn out to be the old foes of pastoral America, the corporations and monopolies.

It was predictable that the first target chosen by the government in its new zeal for nature would be that ancient enemy, Standard Oil, which had polluted the waters of New Orleans. It is also predictable that future policies will not be implemented—any more than the Sherman Act was—to transform the corporate structure. We may expect, instead, ingenious devices for passing on to the consumer the costs of cleanliness.

The wide support commanded by the ecology problem is probably due to its uniquely ecumenical qualities. It is not an issue which provokes class conflict or widens generation gaps. Everybody wants clean air and water and open space. Another soothing feature of ecology is that it promises to remove the growing antagonism toward science evident in the student generation of the Sixties. Students have begun to blow their minds with talk of ecosystems, recycling, and biospheres, apparently unaware that the concept of nature held by most biologists is not that of John Muir, but is as abstract and mathematical as the nature conceived by atomic physicists.

The political implications of the new and benign consensus appear most clearly when it is contrasted with the consensus pursued by the Johnson Administration. It is not accidental that at the same time as the Nixon Administration is using environment to forge a new unity, it has been shelving, retarding, or neglecting most of the previous policies dealing with blacks, the poor, education, and the cities. Johnson's vision of the Great Society lacked nobility, but it never excluded the disadvantaged. The Nixon consensus, by placating the silent majority, is also capitalizing upon the despair of the confused minority of activists who had struggled for racial justice and economic improvement and who now, by their commitment to nature, were tacitly conceding that racial and economic injustice were ineradicable facts of American society.

The evolution of student activism, from the involvement of the Sixties to the pastoral innocence of the Seventies, bespeaks a growing revulsion toward politics. "Our politics," writes Jerry Rubin, is "our music, our smell, our skin, our hair, our warm naked bodies, our drugs, our energy, our underground papers, our vision." His testament, *Do It!*, closes with this vision: "People will farm in the morning, make music in the afternoon, and fuck wherever and whenever they want to." The revulsion against politics is all the sadder because it is being expressed by a generation which taught itself to be the most deeply political one in recent history.

"Let us get America moving again," President Kennedy had exhorted. The struggle of the Sixties demonstrated how difficult and costly that task could be. In casualties, it may be likened to World War I, where Europe lost a whole generation of young men. The high price of change is inherent in the basic features of the political system and its surrounding technological culture.

First, the institutions of our national government have become bureaucratized to an extraordinary degree. They are huge in size, hierarchical in structure, and impersonal in their ways. As they become distended, they also become less amenable to control and coordination. Change is not typically defeated by a bureaucratic conspiracy but by the normal methods of the system. The tendency of any bureaucratic organization is to assimilate an important change of policy into its routine ways of proceeding, with the result that change is accommodated to the needs of the organization, instead of the organization accommodating itself to the demands of change. Add the interlocked bureaucracies of government, business, and the military, and their extension throughout the world and into outer space, and it is apparent why it takes so much to move the system. One must literally move heaven and earth.

Second, since the Civil War, the system has steadily evolved into a mechanism for blurring choices. The party system works to make both parties identify the same issues and define their programs in very similar terms. At the same time, the dynamic supplied by competition between interest groups reinforces the main thrust of the system because the legitimacy of the groups themselves depends upon their accepting the rules of the game and striving for limited, incremental objectives. There is a powerful and persistent mainstream in American politics which fixes the limits of reform. Successful reform movements of the twentieth century, such as the New Freedom and the New Deal, have accepted the prevailing assumptions and proceeded to improve the going system. As others have pointed out, FDR's New Deal did not save capitalism, but it did save the corporations.

Third, the evolution of the American economy into a corporate structure with large-scale and interconnected units of finance and production has been accelerated by the technological revolutions of the twentieth century, especially the revolution in electronics. This development has an important bearing upon the possibilities of change. On the one side, the economy of the technological society is continually in process of innovation. It is governed by a rhythm of incessant change, constantly producing new techniques, equipment, and products. On the other side, technological society has a logic and a set of imperatives which confine change within narrow limits. It needs adaptable, technique-oriented persons to operate its systems. It needs a society which will not cling to traditions and customs. It needs a public which has a bottomless appetite for consumption and whose patterns of need and desire are easily altered. Given the dynamic of change encapsulated in a certain logic, the result is a paradox: a society dominated by the rigidities of change; a society in which constant innovation conceals a persistent direction. The difficulties encountered in changing this type of society are measurable by the apparent impossibility of resolving racial problems, reducing poverty and class inequities, reviving the cities, coping with the destruction of the environment, and redefining education.

This form of society is evolving its own politics, one adapted to the needs of technology. To begin with, the present polarization actually works to the advantage of those who are attempting to govern. The dialectic between left and right provides a dynamic which an uncharismatic President would otherwise lack. The rhetoric, tactics, and demeanor of the young, together with the militancy of some blacks, have activated the right and kept it in motion. The majority may be silent, but they are also resentful, fearful, and ready for mobilization. The tactic of the Nixon Administration is to play off these two dynamics in different ways. The President feeds the fantasies of the right by allowing his Vice President and Attorney General to fulminate and, occasionally, to crack down on dissenters. He gives the right an atmosphere of toughness and the left a few martyrs, while distracting the mass media by crude threats. At the same time, the President moves to undercut the left whenever its objectives are taken over by political moderates. He will champion ecology, guaranteed annual income, a more rational welfare system, and peace in Vietnam. He will then process these causes to the point of blandness so that the right can digest them, while the left remains hungry but unsure of the reasons why.

There are signs that the President is winning the respect of the journalistic connoisseurs of American politics. And those barometers of approaching success, the social scientists, have begun their trips to the back door of the White House. The President is being praised as a shrewd pragmatist who possesses a superb sense of timing and is careful with his political capital. It is possible, however, that what is being admired in the President is more than the politics of opportunism, which is hardly new; it is a new art form growing out of the demands of technological society. Perhaps the cunning of history has brought to the highest office in the land a man whose genius is non-leadership. The President himself has characterized his style as one of low visibility, and has asked for a politics of lowered voices. His ideal seems to be a republic whose public space would be filled by silence, or, at most, by the "lowered profile" of a rarely seen leader, conducting politics for a silent majority.

The new politics reflects the fragilities of technological society. Such a society is made anxious by instabilities and tensions, passions and animosities. As it comes to see itself more and more as a vast electronic circuit, it is tempted to define its unity in nonpolitical language, to seek values like "economic growth" and "clean water" which are safely "above" politics. "Restoring nature to its natural state is a cause beyond party and beyond factions. It has become a common cause of all the people of this country."

Beyond these dimensions, there is another aspect of technological society which has interesting political implications. It is a commonplace that technological society increasingly deprives men of useful and satisfying work. Despite all of the inquiries into the psychology and sociology of factory life, for example, it is evident that there is no way to alter substantially the routinized and uncreative nature of work in the factories. The same is largely true of clerical work and of much that passes for technical and even intellectual work.

This is the future awaiting the increasing numbers of young people who are being educated and encouraged to develop unsatisfiable expectations about their adult roles. A superfluous population is being produced, one that cannot be absorbed and simultaneously fulfilled. Moreover, education is designed to increase dissatisfactions. It encourages self-consciousness and critical awareness, and nourishes hopes of a better life where beauty and dignity are possible.

As yet, technological society has not figured out how to cope with its superfluous human beings. Without being too fanciful one might suggest the following possibility. The governors of the technological order could combine repressive legal measures with a welfare system which would produce euphoric demoralization. Such a welfare system would merely have to extend many elements already present or probable, such as a guaranteed annual income and unemployment compensation. Subsidize the arts so that music would blare throughout the land, and then take the final step of relaxing drug controls. This seems incredible, but no more so than Senator Goldwater urging the relaxation of marijuana laws. When the incredible becomes credible, then the system will have systematically introduced juvenicide as public policy.

VI
Epilogue

SEPTEMBER 3, 1970

What were the major educational changes during the Sixties?

Some of the major assumptions, many of the practices, and most of the myths of higher education were badly shaken. There is no doubt that some transformations took place. There is considerable question, however, whether the transformations provided the foundation for anything enduring.

At many institutions the traditional curriculum has been greatly modified or abandoned in favor of more "experimental" courses. Apart from the occasional vice of promoting non-courses, experimentalism has mainly meant things like encouraging students to initiate courses or to share in formulating them; placing less emphasis upon grades or devising new symbols of performance; adopting an open-minded view of what will be acceptable as "work" in a course; and, in general, making it possible for students to choose the mode and pace of their studies.

The virtue of experimentalism is to have recognized, and to have attempted to break with, the passive character of the "educational process," as it is called, at most institutions, especially at the larger ones. This is a step forward, as virtue usually is, but hardly a revolution. Above all, it evades rather than confronts the great change which has come over the students of the Sixties and which is expressed in their hostility toward curricula designed to prepare them for a "place" in the job structure of society. Many able students plainly want no part of what America has customarily offered its college graduates. Although experimental courses tend to reflect this anti-vocationalism, they also tend to exacerbate the powerlessness which is the lot of those who renounce a vocational calling.

"Student participation" was another of the novelties of the period. The most controversial questions here centered around the matters of faculty appointments and promotion, student admissions, and degree requirements. Now that rhetoric and passions have subsided, it can be clearly seen that neither the great hopes of the challengers nor the great fears of the defenders have been fulfilled.

The most explosive possibilities of "participation" appeared in the controversies surrounding the establishment of black studies programs or departments. There was an evident split between those blacks, on the one side, who looked upon the programs as a way of introducing a neglected subject matter and altering the racial composition of faculties and student bodies and, on the other side, those who conceived the programs as training camps for activists and staging grounds for struggle in the ghetto. It is too early to judge which, if either, of these elements will win, or whether they will remain in tension. It is also too early to determine whether blacks will insist on segregating their programs and personnel, thereby consolidating independent enclaves within the universities, or whether they will consent to one or another form of integration. However this comes out, a truly profound change in American society will have taken place only when black youth can look forward with the same confidence as white youth to college attendance as an almost normal part of growing up.

If there was any one change in American higher education that was visible to all observers, it was the increasing politicization of the campuses. We have already treated this matter at some length, and here we shall only consider why politicization has evoked such widespread apprehension and misgivings. The most common charge is that political activity contaminates the search for truth and jeopardizes academic freedom. Politics means partisanship and partisanship is the enemy of truth.

Rather than attempt to argue that the notion of academic freedom needs to be revised and that revision must be preceded by a more searching inquiry into the nature of politics and of political education, we shall only suggest that in large measure the fears about politicization of the campuses arise out of an unduly narrow conception of politics. This conception faithfully reflects the narrow terms in which Americans have typically talked about and practiced politics. That mode of thought and that practice are major contributing factors to the present crisis of American society.

In America, politics means bargaining and compromise between organized groups for limited and usually material prizes. To most citizens, it means periodically choosing between one or another moderate candidate and one or another blurred issue. Even though the stakes are limited, the rules of the game are many and confining. Hence, small novelties look like major violations. When new actors appear, e.g., blacks or students, employing new tactics and language, and pursuing "ideal" goals, intense fear and hostility are aroused. Such departures are viewed as radical, not because they necessarily are, but because politics itself has been so narrowly conceived, so tightly drawn, that innovation appears as revolution. Americans have always been hospitable to economic innovation but in recent times they have become increasingly suspicious and fearful of creativity in the political realm.

Perhaps the most discussed change on the campuses during the decade was the appearance of that troublesome companion of politics, violence. It is worthwhile remembering that violence was not a part of student politics in the beginning–in fact, it hardly appeared before early 1968. Since then, it has continued to grow.

In order to understand the growth and significance of violence in student politics, it is necessary to distinguish the violence which is overt, spontaneous, and committed by large numbers of people employing mainly the force of their bodies, from the violence which is covert, calculated, and perpetrated by a small handful using manufactured weapons. This latter form of violence, properly called terrorism, is a familiar historical phenomenon. Sometimes it is the expression of personal pathology, and sometimes the product of a totally despairing analysis of the possibility of significant social change. The United States has experienced terrorism before (e.g., by anarchist assassins, Ku Klux Klansmen, and Molly Maguires) but what is disturbing about the new terrorism is that it is done by *young* people. Furthermore, this terrorism is justified in some quarters (e.g., Weathermen) by an ideology brewed from domestic American ingredients. The new terrorism, in short, cannot be dismissed as the work of foreign fanatics inspired by alien doctrines. It represents the last stage of the despair of the young with America.

The mode of violence which we have described as overt, unpremeditated, and collective is closely connected with, even an outgrowth of, the new politics spawned on the campuses—a politics which responds to different rhythms, pursues different ends, and is communicated in a different language from conventional politics. It is pulsating and kinetic, contemptuous of compromise and impatient with routines; and it threatens always to overflow customary channels. It sees victory as something gained by energy and exuberance rather than cunning. Like its insistent music in the background, it is shaped toward a climactic moment. When it encounters certain obstacles, its gathering energy is ready to explode. When confronted by abstract rules and policies, by stolid and anonymous agents of authority, by the rituals which civilized society contrives to defuse passion, it is ready to spill over into provocative and destructive acts.

What are the conditions which produce this kind of violence? In part it arises out of frustrating encounters with a cumbersome and unresponsive system. The frustration grows as the new politics increasingly differentiates itself from the established practices. The system thus appears increasingly unresponsive—not necessarily because it in fact is, but because its challengers have sharpened the distinctions. Eventually the point is reached where the system may in fact respond but the challengers cannot recognize it—just as the system managers may find no sense in the antics of the challengers.

In part, too, this kind of violence is a reaction to the drabness of American politics, a reaction natural in a generation which loves whatever is dramatic, colorful, and provocative. Perhaps (as the cliché goes) we are a violent people; but maybe that is because we have increasingly become a politically unimaginative and conservative people. We now congratulate ourselves on the fact that we are the oldest, most continuous–and therefore–most stable democracy in the world. Violence is a protest against pedestrian politics and stale rhetoric. It becomes a means of turning politics into drama.

Although some of the overt and spontaneous campus violence may be explained by the usual categories of "mob psychology," and although some of it is the work of petulant and spoiled kids, and some more of it originates in black frustration and rage against a white world, it is important to recognize the deeper significance of the assaults on both persons and property.

Students have not attacked the police with guns: it is difficult to find an authenticated instance of actual sniping, much less a case where a student sniper has been convicted in a court of law. They have used clubs, rocks, and their own bodies as weapons. When students assault police, the physical contact becomes a way of asserting that there is a human reality to the world, that the world is not all plastic and steel. If, in Hegel's world, the master and the slave needed each other, in our world perhaps the cop, sealed within his battle jacket and shielded by his visor, needs the student as much as the student needs him.

The mounting assaults against property are correlated with significant changes in the nature and meaning of property. Younger generations have been brought up in a world of replaceable and disposable objects. Property has lost its associations with permanence and stability, just as it has long since lost any direct connection with labor. Important property is institutional property–which is to say the main forms of property are associated with the main forms of power and authority in our society. In either case, whether property is viewed as replaceable or as institutional, it loses sanctity.

The most worrisome aspect of student violence is that it is increasing, which means that it threatens to become an integral part of the new politics; if not a constant feature, then at least an immanent possibility. Student activists, while reluctant to use violence, have been equally reluctant to condemn their "allies" who do use it, be they Angels, Crazies, or Panthers. A certain dulling of sensibilities is bound to result, a loss of sureness about what is morally intolerable. This will lead inevitably to brutalization, to viewing the enemy precisely as he is said to view you: as an object.

Shortly after the last essay in this book was written, American soldiers invaded Cambodia and National Guardsmen killed four students at Kent State University. The campus response was prompt and passionate—the most powerful expression to date of the new politicization.

Cambodia provoked a genuine political uprising on the nation's campuses which has left a range of consequences whose full effects have not yet been fully registered. During the first week of May, about 500 campuses shook off ordinary routines to express their shock and outrage. An uneasy academic year erupted in a storm of political activity. "Before Cambodia," ran a recent memorandum to the President, "many of us on the campuses believed that deep disaffections afflicted only a small minority of students. Now we conclude that [Cambodia] may have triggered a vast pre-existing charge of pent-up frustration and dissatisfaction."

The responses were astonishing. Secretary of State Rogers confessed, with proper diplomatic understatement, that the Administration had not fully anticipated the campus reaction to the invasion. Equally astonishing was the response of politicians and campus officials. With virtual unanimity, college administrators gave ground. They relaxed the normal rules governing academic routines and campus facilities. Several even expressed their sympathy with the antiwar sentiments of the students. National and local politicians were less unanimous, for they had to contend with the fears and hatreds of Middle America which for the past quarter century they had done so much to create. Even so, many politicians urged students and faculties to exert pressure on the government, especially in the campaign to limit the war powers of the President.

More astonishing still was the speed of the about-face of the President and his advisers. They were compelled to repeated justifications of the invasion, justifications so transparent that the public was given an unparalleled opportunity to watch a myth being manufactured. So intense was the pressure that the President soon had to promise that American troops would be pulled out of Cambodia on a specific date. More important, he had to keep that promise, despite the risks. Rarely if ever in American history has a President reacted so hurriedly to a wave of public sentiment and reversed a policy. The reversal was dangerous because it involved a preannounced military retreat accomplished in full view of the entire world and against the opposition of some of his own military men. The reversal was also difficult politically, because it touched strong popular emotions of patriotism and national pride.

This heady experience of campus power may obscure the special circumstances which made it possible and blind the campuses to the gathering political dangers. Even if we grant what is not at all self-evident, that the termination of the Cambodian intervention marks a decisive turn toward disengagement in Indochina, the fact remains that a unique conjuncture of circumstances made the result possible. The power of the antiwar forces in the Senate was cresting while popular support for the President's Vietnam policies was temporarily ebbing. Such a fortuitous conjunction might occur again, but the fact that the success of the campus protest depended upon it demonstrates that its potential falls far short of being revolutionary.

That the campuses had such potential was once an illusion of the radical left. Unfortunately, it is now becoming an illusion held by an ever-increasing number of citizens of all classes and promoted by politicians of both parties. We may even now be moving from a period dominated by the one illusion to a period dominated by the other, the illusion that since a revolutionary peril exists, harsh and systematic measures are therefore needed. Although there have been specific instances of severe force being applied against campuses, there seems as yet no determination on the part of the Nixon Administration to mount a sustained attack upon higher education. Nevertheless, the present campaign against the Black Panthers, as well as the past experience of heresy-hunting, argue that political suppression is not an unthinkable possibility. There is, however, one important difference between suppressing campus political activity and suppressing Panthers, Communists, and alleged faculty "Reds," a difference which presents certain difficulties to policy-makers. The society needs campuses in a way that it does not need Panthers and leftists. As Professor Teller, an archenemy of the new politics put it, if campus disturbances continue, "in 20 years, the United States will be disarmed."

If a systematic campaign were to be launched against the campuses, certain elements would have to be present in combination. What would the profile of such a campaign look like? First, there would have to be a demonstrated willingness to apply police and/or military force against the campuses and to apply it quickly, often, and disproportionately to the actual threat. Second, there would have to be politicians ready to define themselves primarily by their hostility toward higher education, in its intellectual as well as its political aspects; ready to make that hostility a fundamental feature of their electoral campaigns and daily rhetoric; ready to initiate policies or legislation patently designed to injure the operation, development, and morale of campuses and to restrict traditional faculty prerogatives; ready to provoke or maintain campus unrest, thereby proving to the public that a revolutionary conspiracy exists; and careful not to cripple so vital a national resource as the campuses, only to render them docile and powerless.

This combination, in which repression provides the stuff of a political dynamic, does not exist in Washington at the present time. The backlash to Cambodia has produced instead some conciliatory gestures, such as the appointment of Alexander Heard as a temporary Presidential adviser, the creation of a Commission on Campus Unrest, and the acknowledgment that, at times, the rhetoric of the Vice President and Attorney General may have been a bit much. Although nothing profound is likely to happen as a result of any of these moves, they hardly suggest anything ominous.

But in one part of the country the combination of anti-university elements is in active operation. Since 1967 California has been governed by an administration which has perfected the art of using the universities for political advantage. The dynamic of the Reagan administration depends almost entirely upon its ability to sustain public anger against education. In this way not only is he assured of solid public support for his periodic attacks on higher education, but he is also enabled to distract the voters' attention from welfare programs, taxes and revenues, primary and secondary education, and boondoggles like the one of converting the *Queen Mary* into a tourist attraction.

The Reagan administration may have given the illusion of being little more than a Hollywood creation, but behind the appearance is a sure instinct for power. Nowhere is this displayed more clearly than in Reagan's open domination of the Board of Regents, the supreme authority of the nine-campus university system. The Governor's control over the Board is best summarized by the Board's voting patterns. On any matter involving political controversy, be it finances or personnel, he can usually count on a majority of 20 to 4, rarely less than 17 to 7. As now constituted, the Board is deeply conservative and representative mainly of great corporate power and its auxiliarics in public relations, advertising, and the law. The composition of the Board has pretty much been this way for many years. What is new is not the presence of conservatism on the Board, but the disappearance of that possessive and paternalistic affection toward the University which used to temper regental outbursts. Several

Regents plainly do not like the University or its employees.

In the old days Regents used to contend fiercely with governors and legislators over the budget of the University. Now, however, it is a fairly predictable process. It runs like this: the Board prepares its budget and the Governor prepares his. Since the Governor is, at the same time, a member of the Board and since most of its influential members are his appointees, it is fair to say that neither party is very much in the dark about what the other is prepared to concede. Every year the charade is played out and the financial plight of the University steadily worsens, its construction plans halted while student enrollment pressures rise, its faculty salaries lagging well behind those of comparable institutions, until the only promising solution appears to be the one rumored about: that the Regents are thinking of selling a couple of campuses.

It is clear that, during the Sixties, the Regents have lost the autonomy which the California constitution intended they should have.[1] As a result, they have become a conduit of, rather than a buffer against, hostile political forces.[2] Their role as guardians of the financial needs of

---

[1] Article IX, section 9 of the constitution establishes the Board of Regents. It contains the following: "The university shall be entirely independent of all political or sectarian influence and kept free therefrom in the appointment of its Regents and in the administration of its affairs. . . ."

[2] Occasionally the politics of the Regents is expressed amusingly, if spitefully, as when they refused to award an honorary degree to Mayor Lindsay. Berkeley faculty responded by awarding the mayor a citation.

the University has been subordinated to that of an agency for carrying out the politico-fiscal policies of the Governor.[3] The Board of Regents has become incorporated into the political plans of the Reagan administration.

In surveying the actions of the Regents over the past few years, one is tempted to describe them as counter-revolutionary, except for the fact of a revolution which never materialized. Nonetheless, believing that they are combatting revolutionary movements and conspirators, the rulers of the university system have struck at most forms of hopeful change and destroyed or threatened some traditional practices–traditional, that is, at decent colleges and universities. The first major step toward pacification of the campuses was in 1968. The motivation behind it was plainly political. Eldridge Cleaver delivered several lectures in an experimental course held on the Berkeley campus. The Regents declared that academic credit could not be given for the course, even though the course was well under way. They went on to reverse their own well-established principle by which the faculty had been granted authority over curriculum, course credits, and the use of "guest lecturers" in a course.

---

[3] The most vivid illustration occurred during the maneuvering over the 1967-68 budget when the Regents ended up appropriating nearly $25 million from their own special funds to round out an austere budget. The issue is not that universities ought not to dip into their own funds during periods of fiscal troubles, but rather that in this instance the Regents were abetting the generally punitive fiscal policies of an Administration bent on redeeming its campaign rhetoric at the expense of education, welfare services, and medical services. See the account of this dispute in V. A. Stadtman, *The University of California, 1868-1968* (New York: McGraw-Hill, 1970), pp. 493-95.

The Board's next step was to fire faculty members on political grounds, even if it meant violating their own rules. The perfect test case was provided by a young philosopher who had been teaching on a temporary basis and was now about to be offered a regular appointment. The philosopher, Angela Davis, was female, black, an alumna of Brandeis, a student of Herbert Marcuse (who was about to have his own annual reappointment blocked by the Regents), and an avowed Communist. In order to prevent the appointment, the Regents had not only to reject a recommendation from the faculty, but they had to violate their own rules–first, by taking the final disposition of the case from the office of the UCLA Chancellor, where normally it would have been concluded, and, second, by ignoring their own resolution which forbids firing faculty members because of their political views.[4]

All of these complicated maneuvers were prompted by the fact that when the Regents had first discharged this same philosopher, a Los Angeles judge had held that she could not be fired for political reasons. The Regents have won a motion to have the case transferred to another jurisdiction. Such are the whimsies of the law-and-order

---

[4] Later, the Regents declared that the firing was based on Miss Davis's intemperate language, which was interpreted as indicative of conduct unbecoming a faculty member. This justification was produced after the actual decision had been taken. The press and media throughout the state made it public knowledge that Miss Davis would be fired well before the announcement, just as they had reported the daily development of the Regents' argument that she was not being fired for her political views but for her deportment.

mind that one is led to believe that the main difference between the campus rebels and the Regents is that the students break the rules, while the Regents merely change or evade them.

The cynical disregard for the spirit of legal forms is not a peculiarity of California conservatism. We have seen the defenders of law and order prosecuting the Chicago Seven, hunting down the Panthers, and pushing what the President recently called "the necessary strong methods" of quick entry and preventive detention. Doubtless the President was being sincere when he said that "repression . . . is not a government policy," just as the Regents doubtless believe that their recent resolutions are individually tough but not the collective product of a policy aimed at eliminating academic freedom and prerogatives. The predictable result in both cases will be a further decline of authority. Those in high office fail to understand that their own legal lawlessness promotes both the lawlessness they abhor and the political disrespect which feeds so much of the present lawlessness.

Following the campus furor over Cambodia the Regents again began to challenge faculty prerogatives. In July, 1970, a few Regents succeeded in temporarily blocking two faculty promotions, one involving tenure for a young faculty member who had been active in moderate left politics on the Berkeley campus (and who was defended by the Berkeley Chancellor for being a restraining influence), the other a promotion to full professorship for the chairman of Miss Davis's department. At this same meeting the Regents singled out two professors, well-known for their highly conservative views, and granted them exceptional salary increases, thereby prompting one Regent to remark, "We are blocking liberal professors and voting raises for conservatives—how much more political can we get?"[5]

The answer to the last question is, quite a bit. The Regents have made it clear that they are determined to impose tighter "discipline" on the faculty. In this task they have found a willing agent in Charles Hitch, the University's president. According to the latter, the present system of voluntary adherence to a code of faculty ethics has not worked because faculty committees have mistakenly assumed their "main duty to be that of defender of all the rights of the faculty member without a corresponding degree of concern for the welfare of the University" (i.e., such committees have blocked local chancellors in their attempts to fire faculty members for political reasons). He has called for the rules to be revamped so as to prevent teachers from altering course content or from rescheduling courses for political reasons. He has also asked for greater administrative voice in curriculum and course content to protect the "academic freedom of students" by screening out "extraneous subject matter" or "irrelevant discussion." "We are," he noted without irony, "experiencing new pressures."

---

[5] On August 7, 1970, it was announced by one Regent who had blocked the promotions of (as he put it) "the two faculty described in the press as 'liberals' " that the promotions would probably go through. He also defended the exceptional salary increases even though in one case neither the Berkeley Chancellor nor the Berkeley faculty had recommended it. As the Regent noted, the faculty member had "long been a colleague of mine." What seems to have been lost in the dispute is not whether liberal faculty are punished or conservative ones rewarded, but whether the Regents have any business determining complex questions of academic competence.

The recent actions of the President suggest another change of great historical significance. During his presidency Clark Kerr had always managed to preserve considerable autonomy by attracting strong faculty loyalties. But his successor has become wholly dependent on his employers. This historical shift in the President's power was clearly recognized at the Regents' meeting when the President brought in his proposals for faculty discipline. According to newspaper accounts the proposals were received "enthusiastically." One Regent called it "a brave first step" and another suggested that the Regents might some day have to take away all of the Academic Senate's authority "and give it to the president over whom we have control."

The time span of these events does not stretch over several years but is compressed in a short period. Moreover, the pace is quickening and the Regents' offensive is spreading. At their July, 1970, meetings the Regents instructed the chancellors to prepare measures for eliminating "socio-political advocacy" and "the dissemination of lewd, obscene [a bit of California overkill] articles and photographs" from student newspapers. Failing such measures, the Regents promised to cut off all funds to the papers.

When the Berkeley faculty voted to modify ROTC programs, the Regents' response was to approve a resolution to explore the possibility of introducing ROTC units at the four campuses which do not now have them.

After the Berkeley faculty had voted to request the termination of the relationship between the campus and two laboratories which, according to an official report, "encompass every aspect in the process of developing nuclear weapons," and over which the campus had virtually no control, the Regents passed a resolution (July 17, 1970) reaffirming the importance of research for national defense and vowing to continue to sponsor such programs.

What all this adds up to is not a series of attacks, but a roll-back which threatens the modest measure of academic freedom previously enjoyed and promises a greater increase of bureaucratic controls. It represents, too, a denial of all that has happened, not only at Berkeley but throughout the country, between 1964 and 1970.

The picture is made all the bleaker by the progressive demoralization of the faculty. Bugged by students, assailed by Regents, surrounded by a hostile citizenry, feeling the pinch of shortages in research funds and of salary increases denied, they, along with their colleagues at the other campuses, have begun to show signs of capitulation. Not even the mildest protest was registered against the Angela Davis decision by the Berkeley faculty; and even the UCLA faculty has begun to retreat. More ominous, there are signs that an organization of faculty members is being formed to seek ways of ridding the campuses of faculty troublemakers, even if they are tenured members. As one of their spokesmen put it, the position of the academic community is much the same as that of the business community in the Thirties: it has developed abuses which it cannot remedy by itself and hence government intervention is justified.

At this juncture it is difficult to predict how long and how far the present dynamic will go in California. Recently it sputtered slightly when some state legislators demanded an inquiry into alleged improprieties involving the borrowing of University funds by a powerful Regent. Shortly afterward another disclosure hinted at some dubious relations between certain Regents and a land development company working on one of the local campuses. When one of the Regents charged that the Board had "ducked the issue" about the company "because some people have been caught with their hands in the cookie jar," and when he raised questions about the improprieties referred to above, the Board quickly moved on to other things.

But the most immediate question for the campuses in California and elsewhere is, after Cambodia, what? In his memorandum to the President, Chancellor Heard had struggled to shake Mr. Nixon and his advisers by describing the situation as "a national emergency" which "we do not believe that our national government really understands." That lack of understanding was confirmed by the cool reception accorded Heard's eloquent statement.

The most striking, if inadvertent, testimony to the chasm separating the thinking of our national leadership from that of the student generation was contained in a report (July, 1970) by the President's National Goals Research Staff. Its conclusion is a classic statement of the current malaise, for it declared that the President cannot set goals for America. Instead he should provide information so that society can debate what it wants. "A national growth policy" would somehow "evolve in varying pieces," but, thanks to the dynamic nature of events, growth "will probably never be completed" during the Seventies. Somehow, too, it did not seem to worry the NGRS that it had provided a long-winded confession that the highest office in the land could not formulate some vision of the future–a failure which was also explained by the "political" consideration of what the Democrats might do if they were supplied with norms for appraising the President's performance. The Report deliberately avoided any discussion of national goals involving such problems as racism, foreign policy, the plight of the cities, or political suppression.

The most characteristic response to the chasm has been to try to bridge it by assimilating student activism into the structure of traditional pluralistic politics. This was the response embodied in the "Princeton Plan" for encouraging summer political activity and promising a moratorium on classes during the final two weeks of the electoral campaign in the fall. Although many students eagerly welcomed the chance to work for the parties or candidates of their "choice," many of their elders took the cooler view that contact with the "real world" would prove sobering. So during the summer students cut their hair, shaved their chins, shed their jeans, lengthened their skirts–mute testimony to the politics that Americans understand and demand.

Many of the goals now being pursued through electoral politics are so eminently necessary–peace in Vietnam, reasserting constitutional control over the President, and ending racial and political oppression–that criticism inevitably seems ungenerous and obtuse. Yet there is reason to pause over the warnings voiced by some politicians and commentators that the odds are overwhelming that students will be disappointed by the results of electoral politics. This is another way of saying that the system is incapable of responding to powerful protests even when they follow orthodox lines. It is also a way of conceding that what need to be changed are not the actors but the assumptions of the system. An infusion of young blood is not going to alter things: there are always more William Moyerses than Mario Savios.

Even in the midst of the Cambodian protest widespread apprehension began to be expressed about what was likely to happen in the fall. In part there is apprehension because student politics is no longer innocent. It has begat its share of opportunists, hooligans, and ideological thugs. If internal corruption and demoralization increase or if electoral politics becomes the controlling form of "political socialization" they will pretty much end what promise there was in the Cambodian flare-up. The meaning of those events was that politics was taking hold in new places and seeking new forms. During the May and June days many thousands of students who, until then, had had little care for political things were initiated into the new politics. It is too early to assess the staying power of these new recruits or the extent of their understanding of the issues. It is also apparent, not only from the popularity of the Princeton Plan but from the fate of the New Left, that the "system" has lost little of its absorptiveness. The New Left of the past decade has seen its issues adopted by liberals and moderates and its tactics rejected by both moderates and extremists—violence is preferred by the latter, electoral politics by the former.

It remains to be seen whether the crisis of the spring of 1970 amounted to a critical experience which could launch a whole new generation of political activists and a whole new style of political action. A few voices did rise above the anxious but self-congratulatory din of the new converts to the antiwar cause and tried to call attention to the profound crisis in the state. A few others tried to call teachers and students to the large task of redefining the aims and structures of higher education so that we might produce educated men for whom knowledge, personal identity, and public commitment are part of the same quest.

Something new took place on the campuses after Cambodia, but in our day it is the special fate of novelty, even extraordinary novelty, to pass quickly and be forgotten. "I had hoped," one of the astronauts wistfully remarked a year after the moon-landing, "that the impact would be more far-reaching. . . ." It may be that the campus effects of Cambodia will be comparable in the long run to those produced by the civil rights movement. It may also be that the aftermath of Cambodia will confirm that we are truly in an iron cage.